Eco-Architecture

Other Books of Related Interest:

Opposing Viewpoints Series

Global Resources

Current Controversies Series

Urban Sprawl

"Congress shall make
no law . . . abridging
the freedom of speech,
or of the press."

First Amendment to the U.S. Constitution

The basic foundation of our democracy is the First Amendment guarantee of freedom of expression. The Opposing Viewpoints Series is dedicated to the concept of this basic freedom and the idea that it is more important to practice it than to enshrine it.

OPPOSING VIEWPOINTS® SERIES

| Eco-Architecture

Christina Fisanick, Book Editor

GREENHAVEN PRESS
A part of Gale, Cengage Learning

GALE
CENGAGE Learning™

Detroit • New York • San Francisco • New Haven, Conn • Waterville, Maine • London

GALE
CENGAGE Learning

Christine Nasso, *Publisher*
Elizabeth Des Chenes, *Managing Editor*

© 2008 Greenhaven Press, a part of Gale, Cengage Learning.

Gale and Greenhaven Press are registered trademarks used herein under license.

For more information, contact:
Greenhaven Press
27500 Drake Rd.
Farmington Hills, MI 48331-3535
Or you can visit our Internet site at gale.cengage.com

For product information and technology assistance, contact us at

Gale Customer Support, 1-800-877-4253
For permission to use material from this text or product, submit all requests online at
www.cengage.com/permissions

Further permissions questions can be emailed to permissionrequest@cengage.com

Articles in Greenhaven Press anthologies are often edited for length to meet page requirements. In addition, original titles of these works are changed to clearly present the main thesis and to explicitly indicate the author's opinion. Every effort is made to ensure that Greenhaven Press accurately reflects the original intent of the authors. Every effort has been made to trace the owners of copyrighted material.

Cover photograph reproduced by permission of © Walter Geiersperger/Corbis.

LIBRARY OF CONGRESS CATALOGING-IN-PUBLICATION DATA

Eco-architecture / Christina Fisanick, book editor.
p. cm. -- (Opposing viewpoints)
Includes bibliographical references and index.
ISBN-13: 978-0-7377-3996-1 (hardcover)
ISBN-13: 978-0-7377-3997-8 (pbk.)
1. Sustainable architecture. I. Fisanick, Christina.
NA2542.36.E26 2008
720'.47--dc22

2008006572

Printed in the United States of America
1 2 3 4 5 6 7 12 11 10 09 08

Contents

Why Consider Opposing Viewpoints?   **11**

Introduction   **14**

Chapter 1: Is Eco-Architecture Beneficial to Humans?

Chapter Preface   **19**

1. The Basics of Green Homes and Communities   **21**
   Bion Howard

2. Eco-Architecture Is Good for Businesses   **33**
   Rod F. Wille

3. Eco-Architecture Can Be Risky for Businesses   **40**
   Frank Musica

4. Eco-Architecture Can Eliminate Sick   **46**
   Building Syndrome
   Stephen del Percio

5. Sick Building Syndrome Is Due to Job Stress   **52**
   Not Building Conditions
   Alexi Marmot et al.

Periodical Bibliography   **60**

Chapter 2: How Does Eco-Architecture Impact the Environment?

Chapter Preface   **62**

1. Eco-Architecture Will Help the Environment   **64**
   Jeffrey Kaye

2. Eco-Architecture's Benefits to the Environment   **71**
   Are Exaggerated
   Jane Powell

3. Large Houses Can Be Eco-Friendly   **78**
   Claire Anderson

4. Large Houses Cannot Be Eco-Friendly   **89**
Stan Cox

5. Urban Sprawl Can Be Beneficial   **97**
Randall G. Holcombe

6. Urban Sprawl Is Not Beneficial   **104**
Carl Pope

Periodical Bibliography   **111**

Chapter 3: How Can Eco-Architecture Be Encouraged?

Chapter Preface   **113**

1. Building Green Is Becoming Easier   **115**
Patrick W. Rollens

2. Building Green Remains Difficult   **123**
Auden Schendler

3. Eco-Architecture Is Becoming More Attractive   **129**
Alanna Stang and Christopher Hawthorne

4. HOAs Often Ban Eco-Friendly Practices
as Unaesthetic   **137**
Stan Cox

5. The LEED Rating System Helps Create
Greener Buildings   **147**
Taryn Holowka

6. The LEED Rating System's Effectiveness
Is Dubious   **155**
Ted Smalley Bowen

Periodical Bibliography   **165**

Chapter 4: How Is Eco-Architecture Being Implemented?

Chapter Preface   **167**

1. More College Campuses Are Building Green   **169**
   Timothy Egan

2. School Districts Are Learning the Benefits
   of Eco-Architecture   **178**
   Debra Lau Whelan

3. Hospitals Are Going Green to Cut Toxins   **186**
   Laura Landro

4. Greenwashing Remains a Challenge to the
   Green Building Community   **193**
   Philip Mattera

5. Ephemeral Structures Are the
   Ideal Eco-Architecture   **203**
   Jo Scheer

Periodical Bibliography   **209**

For Further Discussion   **210**

Organizations to Contact   **212**

Bibliography of Books   **218**

Index   **222**

Why Consider Opposing Viewpoints?

> *"The only way in which a human being can make some approach to knowing the whole of a subject is by hearing what can be said about it by persons of every variety of opinion and studying all modes in which it can be looked at by every character of mind. No wise man ever acquired his wisdom in any mode but this."*
>
> *John Stuart Mill*

In our media-intensive culture it is not difficult to find differing opinions. Thousands of newspapers and magazines and dozens of radio and television talk shows resound with differing points of view. The difficulty lies in deciding which opinion to agree with and which "experts" seem the most credible. The more inundated we become with differing opinions and claims, the more essential it is to hone critical reading and thinking skills to evaluate these ideas. Opposing Viewpoints books address this problem directly by presenting stimulating debates that can be used to enhance and teach these skills. The varied opinions contained in each book examine many different aspects of a single issue. While examining these conveniently edited opposing views, readers can develop critical thinking skills such as the ability to compare and contrast authors' credibility, facts, argumentation styles, use of persuasive techniques, and other stylistic tools. In short, the Opposing Viewpoints Series is an ideal way to attain the higher-level thinking and reading skills so essential in a culture of diverse and contradictory opinions.

In addition to providing a tool for critical thinking, Opposing Viewpoints books challenge readers to question their own strongly held opinions and assumptions. Most people form their opinions on the basis of upbringing, peer pressure, and personal, cultural, or professional bias. By reading carefully balanced opposing views, readers must directly confront new ideas as well as the opinions of those with whom they disagree. This is not to simplistically argue that everyone who reads opposing views will—or should—change his or her opinion. Instead, the series enhances readers' understanding of their own views by encouraging confrontation with opposing ideas. Careful examination of others' views can lead to the readers' understanding of the logical inconsistencies in their own opinions, perspective on why they hold an opinion, and the consideration of the possibility that their opinion requires further evaluation.

Evaluating Other Opinions

To ensure that this type of examination occurs, Opposing Viewpoints books present all types of opinions. Prominent spokespeople on different sides of each issue as well as well-known professionals from many disciplines challenge the reader. An additional goal of the series is to provide a forum for other, less known, or even unpopular viewpoints. The opinion of an ordinary person who has had to make the decision to cut off life support from a terminally ill relative, for example, may be just as valuable and provide just as much insight as a medical ethicist's professional opinion. The editors have two additional purposes in including these less known views. One, the editors encourage readers to respect others' opinions—even when not enhanced by professional credibility. It is only by reading or listening to and objectively evaluating others' ideas that one can determine whether they are worthy of consideration. Two, the inclusion of such viewpoints encourages the important critical thinking skill of objectively evaluating an author's credentials and bias. This evaluation will illuminate an author's reasons for taking a particular stance on an issue and will aid in readers' evaluation of the author's ideas.

It is our hope that these books will give readers a deeper understanding of the issues debated and an appreciation of the complexity of even seemingly simple issues when good and honest people disagree. This awareness is particularly important in a democratic society such as ours in which people enter into public debate to determine the common good. Those with whom one disagrees should not be regarded as enemies but rather as people whose views deserve careful examination and may shed light on one's own.

Thomas Jefferson once said that "difference of opinion leads to inquiry, and inquiry to truth." Jefferson, a broadly educated man, argued that "if a nation expects to be ignorant and free . . . it expects what never was and never will be." As individuals and as a nation, it is imperative that we consider the opinions of others and examine them with skill and discernment. The Opposing Viewpoints Series is intended to help readers achieve this goal.

David L. Bender and Bruno Leone,
Founders

Introduction

> "Eco-Architecture is by definition inter-disciplinary; it requires the collaboration of engineers, planners, physicists, psychologists, sociologists, economists, and other specialists, in addition to architects."
>
> Wessex Institute of Technology,
> United Kingdom, Organizer
> of Eco-Architecture 2008 Conference

In November 2007 the NBC television network launched its Green Is Universal campaign in which many of its programs and public service announcements focused on raising environmental awareness, specifically targeting the environmental toll of daily activities and regularly used household products. NBC's campaign added to a growing effort by large corporations to publicly acknowledge that the environment is in jeopardy and to encourage consumers to join in the effort to save it. The multibillion dollar building industry has joined this quest as well. Although most eco-advocates are encouraged by this resurgence in green activism, many skeptics remain cautious, arguing that the green building movement is simply a fad that will pass as soon as a more lucrative trend comes along.

Known by a multitude of names, such as green building, eco-friendly architecture, and sustainable building, eco-architecture is a complex approach to designing, constructing, remodeling, and furnishing residential and commercial buildings that takes the environment into consideration. Although some sources trace the roots of green building practices back to the nineteenth century, most researchers point to the 1970s—when a small group of builders and consumers began constructing eco-friendly homes—as the approximate time period when the movement gained momentum in the United States. At the time the market for such structures was limited, and many mainstream builders and prospective home buyers were not aware of or were not interested in green building techniques. A broader interest in eco-architecture began in the late 1980s as the impact of buildings on the environment and an overall interest in preserving the natural world intensified. Recognizing a need, the building industry coined the phrase "green building" in the early 1990s and began investing in the movement in earnest.

Many sources credit the launch of the United States Green Building Council's Leadership in Energy and Environmental Design (LEED) guidelines in 1998 for the most recent surge in the interest in eco-architecture. Since then, the market for green buildings and supplies has grown exponentially. McGraw Hill Construction reported a 20 percent increase nationwide in environmentally responsible construction from 2004 to 2005. Most critics point to LEED and other third-party green building guidelines, such as those developed by the National Association of Home Builders and Green Globes, as the main reason for these remarkable gains.

Some activists, however, are reluctant to agree that these guidelines alone are enough to sustain sound eco-friendly building practices. After all, following these guidelines remains voluntary across much of the nation. Indeed, despite the incredible recent growth in the green building industry, only 12 percent of all new single-family dwellings built in 2006 qualified for the U.S. Environmental Protection Agency's EnergyStar designation. Yet, building industry leaders and organizations argue that mandating green construction guidelines will not be beneficial in the long run. According to Todd Meyers of the Competitive Enterprise Institute, "Such market interventions reduce the incentive and pressure for standards to adapt and change to meet the demands of the market.

Shortsighted government policies threaten to impede the more efficient competitive process."

Although it is becoming cheaper and easier to use certified green building materials, green building practices have not become fully integrated into the way most builders and consumers think about architecture. Liz Redman, columnist for *Sustainable Industries*, argues that "the best thing the 'green wave' can do is help society weave concepts of environmental sustainability into daily life." Unfortunately, this revolution in thinking has not arrived to the extent that all building is automatically green building. *Green Builder* found that just over half of all builders say that they regularly use green building practices and supplies in new construction. Many more could be making green building a reality in their businesses but haven't taken that leap yet.

Still, even if many in the building industry have not made eco-friendly practices standard, most of the professionals that populate this field are thinking more seriously about it than ever before. In a 2007 survey conducted by *Professional Builder* magazine, 67 percent of builders disagreed that the green building movement is a fad. In addition, as Matt Gagne notes in the *Bellingham Business Journal*, "Architecture and construction firms are gathering the know-how it takes to work on such projects. . . . Perhaps the most telling sign that the trend is here to stay is those practices are becoming less specialized and more the norm."

The McGraw Hill study estimates that the market for "true" green homes will increase from $2 billion in 2007 to $20 billion in 2012. The authors in *Opposing Viewpoints: Eco-Architecture* debate whether and how that goal may be achieved in the following chapters: Is Eco-Architecture Beneficial to Humans?, How Does Eco-Architecture Impact the Environment?, How Can Eco-Architecture Be Encouraged?, and How Is Eco-Architecture Being Implemented? Clearly, even if green building is a fad that will wane over time, there is certainly money to be made in the interim.

CHAPTER 1

Is Eco-Architecture Beneficial to Humans?

Chapter Preface

According to the U.S. Environmental Protection Agency (EPA), indoor air quality (IAQ) can be two to five times worse than outdoor air quality. It is no wonder, then, that green building practices appeal to consumers. After all, industry leaders market their green products and building techniques as providing safe and healthy living conditions. Even the Centers for Disease Control and Prevention (CDC) has turned its focus to indoor dangers with the recent launch of its Healthy Home Initiative, a program that aims to prevent diseases associated with substandard and otherwise unsafe housing. At the same time, however, questions remain about the evidence linking illnesses to indoor pollutants and the effectiveness of green building efforts in reducing them.

The CDC reports that "childhood lead poisoning, injuries, respiratory diseases such as asthma, and quality of life issues have been linked to the more than 6 million substandard housing units nationwide." Most of the blame for poor IAQ is placed on building materials, such as carpeting, paint, adhesives, and treated wood. Many of these products contain volatile organic compounds (VOCs), which have been linked to cancers and other diseases. Because green building techniques use low- and no-VOC materials, they can improve the quality of indoor air. In addition, the performance and availability of low- and no-VOC products have increased dramatically in the last decade, making them a viable choice for most builders and consumers.

Skeptics wonder whether green building products and techniques can really improve the health of building occupants given that most supporting evidence is anecdotal. As Sustainable Solutions Corporation admits, "These benefits of green building are difficult to quantify but have been reported by many residents, employees, and employers." Although studies are underway to gather more scientific evidence of the health benefits of green buildings, all consumers can do is rely on green building guidelines to ensure that their homes and businesses are being built with their best interests in mind. However, as a recent study for the National Center for Healthy Housing has shown, "there is significant variation in the degree to which national green guidelines consider occupant health."

Ultimately, responsibility for IAQ falls largely on the occupants. In a *Professional Remodeler* article, Glen Salas reminds home builders that "while quality building practices make a huge difference, the occupants of the home control the quality of their indoor air long after the builder is gone." He recommends that they explain to their customers the importance of using eco-friendly cleaning products, closing their windows when they cut the grass, wiping and removing shoes before coming inside, and brushing pets regularly and outdoors. As this debate and the ones taken up by the viewpoints in this chapter demonstrate, the overall impact of eco-architecture on humans is yet to be determined. Although the general sense is that green building products and techniques are certainly better than most alternatives, the actual benefits are still being investigated.

"The overall environmental impact of new building and community development . . . is very important."

The Basics of Green Homes and Communities

Bion Howard

In the following viewpoint Bion Howard, an environmental scientist and former home builder, describes the basic qualities of green homes and communities. He focuses on sustainability and argues that the decisions consumers and home-building companies make about how new homes are built and how old homes are refurbished can have a great impact on everyday life and the future of the planet. He cites energy efficiency, freshwater efficiency, improved indoor air quality, respect for the building site, and reduced environmental impact as reasons why consumers choose to build green.

As you read, consider the following questions:

1. About how many pounds per year does the average U.S. consumer use of "active" materials, according to Howard?

Bion Howard, "Green Building: Builders, Consumers and Realtor' Primer," *Building Environmental Science and Technology (B.E.S.T)*, 2006. www.energybuilder.com/greenbld.htm. Reproduced by permission.

2. What are the four R's of green building, as cited by the author?

3. New homes today are how much more energy efficient than homes built prior to 1976, in Howard's opinion?

Green Buildings are *really resource efficient buildings* and are very energy efficient, utilize construction materials wisely—including recycled, renewable, and reused resources to the maximum extent practical—are designed, constructed and commissioned to ensure they are healthy for their occupants, are typically more comfortable and easier to live with due to lower operating and owning costs, and are good for the planet. The overall environmental impact of new building and community development and the choices made when we either re-use or demolish existing structures is very important. . . .

What Is Sustainability?

The term "sustainable" is bandied about with great elan [eagerness] these days; so what does it mean?

Paraphrased from a *United Nations Environmental Programme* Document:

> '. . . *meeting the needs of people today without destroying the resources that will be needed . . . by persons in the future; based on long range planning and the recognition of the finite nature of natural resources . . .*'

In the definition, there is no exclusivity of human-kind, and therefore in broad terms it can represent the protection of resources utilized by all living organisms on the planet. This meaning while broad, does not exclude humanity from utilizing natural resources, whether renewable or fixed, but rather calls for more effective management of our resource utilization so as not to harm the planet or future possible users or uses of our resources. . . .

Environmentally sensitive development at all levels—housing, commercial, institutional, infrastructure—appears to be a very promising approach to help achieve sustainability in these terms. Humanity shares a common need for affordable, healthy, durable, comfortable housing and workspaces designed and built to maintain or uplift the human condition. Unfortunately, as a general criterion, this does not yet frequently occur as a rule throughout the World.

Some corporate leaders—such as 3M, Dupont, Amoco, Carrier, Trane, and others—have begun in earnest to recognize the market value of environmentally sound products and manufacturing approaches. Over the next 10 to 20 years, accelerated movement toward a more sustainable economy and infrastructure will be needed, to head off environmental problems such as global climate change, enlargement of the Ozone "hole," possible foodchain disruption and depletion of ocean fisheries, top-soil depletion and erosion, desertification, and ground water contamination. . . .

Why Buy a Green Home?

There are many questions consumers have about environmental products. Do they really work as promised? Why bother to look for and purchase an environmental product? Can my shopping decisions really make a difference and help the planet? The answer—especially for our homes and the products they entail—is a resounding yes.

U.S. consumers utilize greater resources per capita than any other people worldwide. We [use] about 20,000 pounds (10 tons) per person per year of "active" materials. These include virgin forest products, fuels, steel, glass, cement and plastics. An astounding 90 percent of these of materials becomes "waste" in less than one year, according to a 1992 study by the US Office of Technology Assessment (OTA). Residential construction processes are still fairly inefficient compared to other industries according to these OTA reports to Congress.

Home building needs to undergo a process of technological substitution and rethinking to become more environmentally sensitive and sustainable. In a green housing project, many inefficiencies are addressed and overcome, so your home becomes part of the solution. The building industry is acting to incorporate the growing knowledge of green buildings into housing products and services, but consumer demand plays an important role in getting these better products to market.

As a Nation we consume over 2 *billion* tons of non-durable resources each year. Add to this quantity: non-hazardous industrial waste equaling 11 *billion* tons per year (OTA said 6.5 billion tons could be reduced by design decisions and enhanced recycling), 1.9 *billion* tons per year of pollution from automobiles and light trucks, 700 *million* tons of hazardous waste, about 600 *million* tons of building related air-pollution, and 180 *million* tons of municipal solid waste (sewerage sludge, etc.). . . . Our productive economy produces these by-products of our affluent life-style, which are threatening our environment.

Luckily, our homes can become a powerful tool that empowers us to help protect the environment. When we live in a green home we encourage reducing waste, implementing recycling, using renewable materials and energy sources, and implementing a better way of producing housing. These are the Four-R's: *Reduce, Recycle, Renewable and Rethinking*. When our homes are built or remodeled with these important tools in mind, each one becomes an "engine" pulling to help the environment. . . .

Green Homes Are Very Energy Efficient

New homes today are about 35% more energy efficient than those built prior to 1976. However, they need to be more so to deliver the best economics for buyers. Why? Simple really—your home is the biggest purchase of your life and it should not have the biggest impact on your pocketbook from utility bills, or the environment from energy waste. . . .

Very basic materials, building techniques, and designs distinguish an energy efficient home. Sealing up air-leaks like construction cracks and holes is very important. Increased attic, wall and foundation insulation, and installing high-performance windows and better doors completes the building "shell." Using efficient electric lighting and plug-in appliances, and upgrading to high efficiency furnaces, heat-pumps and boilers further reduces energy waste. A floor plan and building orientation designed to admit winter solar heat, ample day lighting, and avoid summer-time sun further reduces energy waste. Such a "package" may save up to 65% in your green home versus a typical homes' utility bills. As with many quality oriented projects, energy efficiency upgrades perform best when installed as a package by professionals. However, some projects like insulating your attic, putting on weather-stripping, and installing a digital clock-thermostat are simple and low-cost do-it-yourself measures. . . .

Water Efficiency

Water is one of our most precious natural resources. Homes use hundreds of gallons each day which could be conserved or saved as "gray-water" to be recycled to water gardens. In a green home, simple and low-cost measures are taken that reduce water use by about half compared to homes constructed in the 1980's. Water saving is important since in many areas fresh water resources are being rapidly depleted by development; with shrinking reservoirs and dropping aquifer depths where wells run dry.

Low-flush toilets, well insulated hot water piping, low-flow shower heads and faucets, and dishwashers and clothes washers that have "water-miser" features are all important to lower home water use. How the hot water is produced is important too. One way to cut down running the tap to get hot water is to install a main solar heated tank to provide year-round warm water, and then use a instantaneous or "tankless" water heater near each point of hot water use. Another useful option is using plumbing planned so that the shortest possible length of pipe runs from the water heater to each hot water–using device or tap.

Landscaping using native plants with high drought resistance is another great way to lower water waste outdoors. Most green architects and home builders have learned what plants flourish with little or no watering, or get assistance from their local university or agricultural extension service to select plants needing little water. Selecting a drought resistant grass, and using lawn chemicals and fertilizer sparingly also reduces watering needs. Grass that is heavily fertilized needs two to four times the water to survive, and may wind up with a weak root system.

Good Indoor Environmental Quality

Indoor environmental quality is a mixture of the air your breathe, the lighting from indoors and outside, noise levels, and even the electromagnetic fields produced by electric power-consuming devices. All these factors contribute to our health, comfort and a sense of well being at home. Bad smells, excessive noise, humming from lights or appliances, and pollutants (*particles, spores, volatile gases or unburned fuel*) all can lead to irritation, poorer health, reduced productivity and, in extreme cases, injury or death.

The basic design, building materials used, and operating efficiency of your green home can help greatly reduce the threat to you and your family of indoor environmental problems. A green home is designed, constructed, and can be easily maintained to be free of unhealthy levels of indoor air pollutants—such as Radon gas, excess moisture, mold and mildew, formaldehyde, passive tobacco smoke, particles and dust-mite allergen (feces)—that can impact occupant health. Once you move in, use the information provided by your green builder or remodelor to properly maintain healthy indoor environments.

In existing homes, owners should check for lead-based paint and have drinking water tested in case lead solder was used to fit the plumbing. Inexpensive kits are widely available for home testing of radon, lead levels, VOC [volatile organic compounds], and drinking water. Also, requesting the seller or remodeler certify that no asbestos was used in the home or in any projects done at your home carries value into the future in terms of health and resale value. In general, states have been gradually moving toward greater disclosure of indoor pollution sources—like radon, lead and asbestos—over the last several years. Your realtor will be able to advise you on local regulations, and can help you obtain information on these matters from sellers or your new home builder.

Once major sources of air pollution indoors are addressed, it is still a good idea to ventilate homes to ensure good comfort and health. American homes have largely been "accidentally" ventilated by leaks through which air flows due to wind pressures and temperature differences. This sometimes results in stuffy or unhealthy conditions. Today, better energy efficiency reduces the leaks and hence "accidental" ventilation may not be enough for comfort. Low cost ventilation techniques include a wide range of fresh-air systems that boost indoor air quality while not adding very much to energy bills. In very cold or hot/humid areas air-to-air heat recovery ventilators ("*heat-exchangers*") provide ventilation at reduced overall energy cost since they reclaim heat or cooling from stale indoor air being exhausted outside. Builders trained in energy efficient construction have been informed how to ventilate homes better with these systems, which can be "tuned" to your climate for least cost and best performance.

If there are allergy sufferers in the household, installing a higher efficiency air-filter element, or an "electrostatic" air fil-

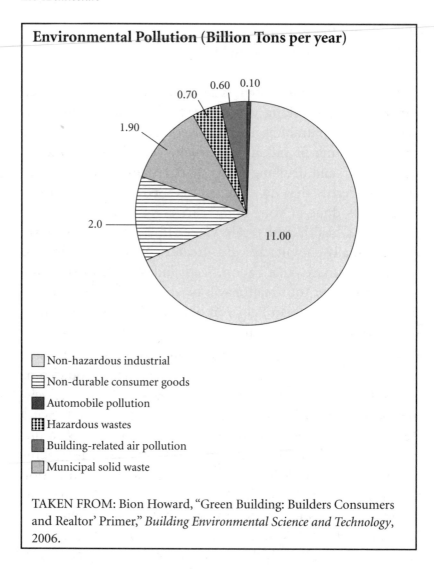

Environmental Pollution (Billion Tons per year)

0.70 0.60 0.10

1.90

2.0

11.00

☐ Non-hazardous industrial
⊟ Non-durable consumer goods
■ Automobile pollution
▦ Hazardous wastes
■ Building-related air pollution
☐ Municipal solid waste

TAKEN FROM: Bion Howard, "Green Building: Builders Consumers and Realtor' Primer," *Building Environmental Science and Technology*, 2006.

ter device, can reduce their discomfort. But one of the biggest advantages of energy efficient construction for allergy sufferers is the lower air leakage, and hence fewer spores, pollen grains and less dust that gets in from outdoors. According to EPA [Environmental Protection Agency] and the CPSC [Consumer Product Safety Commission] such filters may not be necessary in most homes, once the sources of indoor pollutants—especially particles, smoke, and dust-mite allergen—are reduced. Air filters do little to protect against radon gas, pesticides, formaldehyde or other chemical agents.

Specific healthy home information including recommendations you can pass on to builders, designers and remodelors is available from groups like the *American Lung Association*, the Consumer Product Safety Commission (CPSC), as well as the US Environmental Protection Agency and the Department of Energy.

Green Buildings Respect the Site

Your green home has been designed with greater respect for the natural resources on the land. The well designed building site lets natural energy sources work for you—such as solar heating, natural cooling breezes, and placement of vegetation and water bodies nearby. Existing homes will benefit by landscaping too, since planting's can help compensate for poor building orientation, shelter existing homes from winter winds and reduce glaring summer sun which adds to your air-conditioning loads. These steps are free in the planning phase, and research shows they can significantly reduce energy used for air-conditioning and heating homes. Experience designing, building and testing "passive" solar heated and cooled homes indicates simple no-cost/low-cost planning of orientation and window placement can save 20% to 35% on winter heating bills and also can reduce air-conditioning loads.

Designers take advantage of shading and breezes from adjacent buildings and trees, and from carefully considering the surface colors of [objects] nearby the home (walkways, parking lots, etc.) to reduce summer temperatures. Planting new trees, shrubs and ground covers to reduce cold winds washing heat from home surfaces while admitting ample sunlight reduces heating bills and brightens a home in winter.

In summer, deciduous trees along a Southwest to Northwest aspect can reduce the impact of solar heat gains during hot afternoon hours. Studies at Florida Solar Energy Center and Arizona State University have shown building orientation, overhangs and shading, surface colors and textures, and proper planning of landscape vegetation can greatly reduce air conditioning loads.

Reduced Environmental Impact

Many construction materials—such as cellulose and some mineral fiber insulation, steel "stud" framing, manufactured and structural wood products, and sheathing for building exteriors—are now made from recycled, renewable, and reused materials in concentrations ranging from 25% to nearly 100% in their overall content of recycled materials. Where performance, durability, energy efficiency and cost trade-offs appear reasonable, using such materials boosts overall energy efficiency, can greatly benefit the environment, and creates jobs and markets for such materials.

Green building designers and builders also become familiar with local sources of construction materials, such as wood, insulation, windows, concrete block, brick, gravel, etc. Using local materials whenever possible reduces excess energy use from transporting materials long distances and helps local economies by increasing jobs and keeping cash-flows and tax revenues in your community. . . .

Ties to the Community

How many times have you seen advertisements for "affordable housing" only to find it located miles from essential health services, schools, stores, public transportation, or even lacking in fire and police authority? The costs of coping with an "affordable" home in an outlying area requiring long commutes, and big driving distances to shopping, schools, doctors, and recreation sites can cost you over $9000 per year according to estimates by NRDC [Natural Resources Defense Council].

Housing affordability is an overall consideration of all the costs of ownership, not just those costs leading up to putting the key in the front door after closing. Lower first-cost housing that forces you to drive more, requires expensive new utility infrastructure (which you pay for in higher taxes) or is isolated by distance or lack of local social and community services is not really "affordable" when you add it all up. Living in such areas takes a toll on scarce human energy, our emotions, and spare time.

Worse for the environment is the excess fuel-energy required for transportation. The vehicle-miles traveled by persons coping with life in fringe areas escalate compared to well planned communities. In many developing areas political pressures permit developers to avoid contributing large shares of direct costs for adding "infrastructure"—the roads, bridges, water mains, sewers, power-lines—needed to provide essential services to your new home.

In theory this added infrastructure will be developed (long) after the new housing is erected, using funding from the new tax base (your tax dollars). Thus, your new "affordable" home may suffer power outages, traffic congestion, poor water quality, lack of civil services, and other disadvantages while you have to pay higher taxes to compensate for poorly planned development. All these factors can hurt the environment through energy waste, hasty planning decisions, and long lasting impacts on wetlands and open spaces.

Considering a closer location, better knit with community services, can actually save money in the long run, even at higher initial home prices. Unfortunately, drive-distances and other costs of living in fringe areas are not yet recognized factors accounted for in qualifying mortgages. But, unnecessarily high monthly commuting costs take money out of homeowners' pocketbooks that might otherwise pay the mortgage, buy food, or [be] save[d] for college education. Looking for a closer-in or well planned community where schools, libraries, places of worship, and safety services are closely integrated with housing development has environmental advantages. Living with walk-able distances to shopping and community activities can make a large difference in your quality of life.

Social studies have indicated residents of environmentally planned communities are happier, healthier and more productive. Added benefits are lower crime rates and better environmental quality which result due to less dependence on cars (which have been shown to isolate people) and the greater sense of "belonging" to a community.

"A quality green office complex can be
built at a competitive first cost and ...
reap ... future benefits."

Eco-Architecture Is Good for Businesses

Rod F. Wille

Rod F. Wille is a senior vice president at Turner Construction Company, an international general builder, and a Leadership in Energy and Environmental Design (LEED) Accredited Professional. In the following viewpoint, Wille argues that choosing to build green makes good business sense. While the upfront investments for green building modifications such as dual-flush toilets and solar panels might seem costly, he contends that those initial investments are recouped within a short period of time and save companies money over the long term. He cites a number of recent business successes with going green, including Genzyme and Toyota's South Campus.

As you read, consider the following questions:

1. How does integrated design differ from traditional unilateral Design, according to Wille?

Rod F. Wille, "The Business Case for Building Green," *NAIOP's Development Magazine*, Winter 2003. The NAIOP web site is continually updated with up-to-date information about green/sustainable developments. It can be viewed at www.naiop.org. Reproduced by permission.

2. As related by the author, how much money did the Fred Hutchinson Cancer Research Center save from using integrated design techniques?

3. As of 2003, according to Wille, what was the largest building in the United States to receive a LEED gold certification?

It's a given that green buildings are environmentally aware, energy-conscious and generally healthier places to live and work. More recently, however, with advances in design and technology, as well as a plethora of new products available at more competitive prices, green buildings have become solid economic investments.

Moreover, the sustainable design movement has progressed beyond its early market segments of public and educational projects to a broad range of building types that now include commercial, industrial, healthcare and R&D [research and development] facilities.

From a builder's perspective, several of the advantages of green buildings are quantifiable and have been proven on green projects that Turner Construction has recently built.

Recovering Up-Front Costs

Consider the recovery of higher up-front costs on an 18-story commercial office building in the Northeast that used "dual flush" water closets, for example, instead of standard toilets that consume 1.6 gallons of water per flush. The "dual flush" unit cost an additional $540 for the fixture and labor to install it, for a total first cost premium of $97,200 (10 toilets/floor times 18 floors).

If one assumes that 50 percent of the time only one flush will be used on the "dual flush" fixtures, the annual savings is 360,000 gallons of water or approximately $10,000/year in water and sewer cost savings. With a nine-year payback on the first cost premium, and annual savings of $10,000 thereafter, this green feature would make good economic sense (and conserve a significant amount of a natural resource).

On the 624,000-square-foot Toyota South Campus office development in Torrance, California, Turner installed 53,000 square feet of rooftop photovoltaic panels that can generate 550 kw [kilowatts] of electricity, or about 20 percent of the building's total energy usage. Designed to shave peak demand in the summer cooling season, the savings from reduced reliance on the grid will take about seven years to pay back the first cost investment of $1.6 million, according to Toyota executives.

Integrated Design

Integrated design is another significant advantage of a sustainably designed building. An integrated design differs from the traditional unilateral approach of an architect drawing the exterior wall, the engineer designing the mechanical and electrical systems, the interior designer creating the interior environment and the construction manager pricing each component separately. Now, through modeling and other design methodologies, the entire building can be analyzed for energy, esthetics, indoor environment, first cost and life cycle cost. In this way, building owners can make an informed decision early on in the design on how best to invest their money.

An integrated design led to significant cost savings on two recent projects for the Fred Hutchinson Cancer Research Center in Seattle, Washington, totaling 898,000 square feet. The designers took a holistic building approach by analyzing the thermal characteristics of the building envelope, incorporating an interstitial [enclosed] space between floors for access to mechanical and electrical systems, incorporating a high level of automation (sensors for temperature, light and motion) and using very high efficiency equipment throughout.

This "integrated" design resulted in "integrated" savings: $1.9 million in one-time utility company rebates, $850,000 per year in utility savings (electricity and water) and $700,000 per year in operational efficiency savings (i.e, fewer operating engineers needed due to interstitial space and automation).

Specialized Products and Natural Daylight

New technologies to create greener buildings are being developed at an accelerated rate, as manufacturers either modify existing products or develop new ones that conserve more energy, are less detrimental to the environment and enhance the health and well-being of building occupants. This helped solve previous problems of lack of competition, lack of availability and long lead times for delivery.

For example, there are now more than 25 reputable manufacturers of low (or zero) VOC (volatile organic compound) paint. VOC emissions from paints and coatings are indoor air contaminants that are odorous and potentially irritating and/or harmful to the comfort and well-being of building occupants, as well as to the installers of these products. As a result, designers can now specify low VOC products that are high quality, competitive in cost (to "standard" paint) and readily available in the marketplace.

On a current Turner project, the executives at Genzyme in Cambridge, Massachusetts, decided that the health and well-being of the workers in their proposed 300,000-square-foot world headquarters was a high priority. As a result, the designers were asked to bring natural daylight into each occupant's workplace.

Technology allowed for a system of seven heliostat deflecting mirrors on the roof to track the sun's position and divert sunlight into the central atrium. Additional operable sunshade prisms were installed to reflect direct sunlight while allowing diffused daylight to enter the atrium and adjacent offices. On the perimeter facade, a real-time weather station monitors sunlight conditions and controls automated blinds that bring daylight into perimeter offices. Clearly, these systems were a first cost premium, but in addition to the aforementioned health and well-being benefits, there will be a significant energy savings via the use of natural daylighting as well as a potential increase in worker productivity.

Using LEED Guidelines

A key advantage of green building is the use of best practices to achieve more predictable results. For those owners looking for a green roadmap, the Leadership in Energy and Environmental Design (LEED) rating system developed by the U.S. Green Building Council (USGBC) allows a project team to track sustainability throughout design and construction. . . . Version 2.1 makes it easier for the team to tabulate the green results and qualify the project for certification.

There are very helpful design guidelines in the group's "reference package" that allow for the efficient design of cost-effective green strategies. When followed, LEED will achieve the predictable result of a quality sustainable building.

Other owners may opt for a less formal approach, which can also achieve a very high quality green building. The key to success is to retain designers, consultants and a construction manager early on in the planning to develop a feasible, cost-effective, sustainable concept via an integrated design approach. An eco-charrette [design session] held during the conceptual stage of a project allows all stakeholders to brainstorm ideas that evolve into the ultimate design.

Having a financial representative involved will allow the message of life cycles and value analyses to be delivered to the ultimate decision makers. There is no reason that a well-conceived, well-designed green building project should not make good economic sense, when all subjective and objective factors are considered.

Toyota Makes Economic Sense

One Turner project that exemplifies a solid business case for green buildings is the Toyota South Campus project. This of-

Ten Studied Advantages of Sustainable Design

The U.S. Green Building Council (USGBC) published a synopsis of a roundtable forum that was convened at the request of the Environment and Public Works Committee of the U.S. Senate. Entitled "Making The Business Case For High Performance Buildings," the publication outlined 10 advantages of a sustainably designed building:

- Higher up-front costs (if any) for high performance green buildings can be recovered.

- Integrated design lowers ongoing operating costs.

- Better buildings equate to higher employee productivity.

- New technologies enhance occupant health and well-being.

- Healthier buildings can reduce liability.

- Tenants' costs can be significantly reduced.

- Property value will increase.

- Many financial incentive programs are available.

- Communities will notice a developer's efforts.

- Using best practices yields more predictable results.

Some of these advantages are measurable, and others, while somewhat intangible, are gaining credibility in the industry. For example, studies have been conducted that have measured increased worker productivity of up to 26 percent in buildings with high indoor environmental quality. Retail sales have been shown to increase by up to 40 percent when natural daylight is brought into sales areas.

Rod F. Wille, NAIOP's Development Magazine, *Winter 2003.*

fice building achieved a LEED Gold certification (the largest building in the U.S. to receive this rating) and yet was built and fitted out at costs competitive with other local build-to-suit office buildings.

According to Bob Pitts, group vice president, administrative services, Toyota Motor Sales, USA, Inc., the project had to cost less than the average office space lease Toyota was already paying for rental space in Torrance.

Turner, along with LPA Architects, evaluated trade-offs such as a tilt-up concrete panel façade (in lieu of custom-designed curtainwall) that allowed for the first cost premium of rooftop photovoltaic panels. Long-term operating savings were also on Toyota's radar screen when they approved the use of high efficiency air handling equipment and central gas-fired chillers that achieved energy savings well beyond California's stringent Title 24 energy code. Through good planning, Turner was able to recycle 96 percent of the construction waste at an actual savings when compared with sending combined waste to local landfills.

Other green features include use of extensive daylighting, an average of 50 percent recycled content in overall building materials, including structural steel, drywall and ceiling tiles, refurbishable carpet (that will avoid landfills) and even chair webbing made of seat belt remnants.

And now for the really good news: core/shell construction cost $63 per square foot—vs. a local market range of $54 to $76—and interior construction cost $26 per square foot—vs. $22 to $40 in other local buildings. Clearly, the Toyota South Campus project demonstrates that a quality green office complex can be built at a competitive first cost and, in addition, reap the future benefits of energy savings and a high quality of life.

| "*Misunderstanding risks of sustainable design can result in a flow of red ink on the design firm's balance sheet.*"

Eco-Architecture Can Be Risky for Businesses

Frank Musica

In the following viewpoint Frank Musica, a risk management attorney based in Chevy Chase, Maryland, acknowledges that there are many benefits to incorporating sustainable features in constructing new buildings. He warns, however, that the legal risks might outweigh the benefits for design professionals. Given that sustainable design standards come from many sources and are often contradictory, consumers often hold misconceptions about the benefits of eco-architecture, he maintains. As a result, design professionals may be exposed to legal liability if clients feel that their expectations are not fulfilled.

As you read, consider the following questions:

1. What are the goals of sustainable design, in Musica's opinion?

2. As stated by the author, what are "social cost reductions"?

Frank Musica, "Green Design Can Cause Red Ink," *ASHRAE Journal*, vol. 47, December 2005, pp. 116–17. Reproduced by permission.

3. In what ways could a design firm be accused of violating implied or expressed warranties, according to Musica?

Sustainable building design and construction often is promoted as a cost-savings measure. The literature routinely states that the original investment will be paid back within a relatively short time. The picture created by the marketing of sustainable projects is often inconsistent with the end result or leads the owner to believe that cost savings will be significant and easily realized.

In reacting to the trend for sustainable building design, many, and often conflicting, measures of sustainability have been developed. These present increasing and often conflicting challenges to the design community.

Sustainable Design Standards

Sustainable design can be based on many prescriptive "standards" promulgated by groups competing for the leadership position in sustainable design. One of the dominant systems is the United States Green Building Council's (US-GBC) Leadership in Energy and Environmental Design (LEED) rating system. Projects can achieve levels of certification based on awarded points.

With LEED the concept of sustainability became calculable by design professionals and by owners who like to count points. LEED's stated goal is to distinguish building projects demonstrating a commitment to sustainability by meeting the "highest performance standards." The system defines itself as setting "a national standard for achieving high performance, energy efficient and economically viable buildings that enhance occupant well-being through the application of sustainable design principles."

However, what may be inspirational for HVAC [heating, ventilation, and air-conditioning systems] and other designers may seem like a guarantee to project owners.

Generally, clients pursue measurable sustainable design for their buildings because they desire the outcome to be a better product. They may desire the public relations value of a sustainability rating and believe it will increase market value, command higher rents, cut energy costs and lead to reduced employment expenses.

Typical design usually only meets the minimum code requirements regarding energy, water, waste, etc. Sustainable design takes a different approach. The goals are resource efficiency, a protected environment, and healthy conditions for the building occupants. In attempting to reach the goal, design professionals may increase their exposure to legal liability.

Sustainable building design and construction often is promoted as a cost savings measure. The literature routinely states that the original investment will be paid back within a relatively short time. The picture created by the marketing of sustainable projects is often inconsistent with the end result and leads the owner to believe that cost savings will be significant and easily realized.

Risks to Design Professionals

One significant risk centers on the hard-to-measure savings of "social cost reductions." These include higher productivity rates and fewer absences due to illnesses. These types of "savings" hold out a real benefit to project owners or tenants, although they often add little to the bottom line. If the anticipated savings do not materialize, the owner or tenant may look to the designer to make up the "loss."

A significant mistake an engineer can make is to accept a new product based solely on the manufacturer's product data sheets and sales literature. The owner must be informed of the risks inherent in specifying new materials.

Most building systems and products are subject to the Uniform Commercial Codes' four-year limitation on product liability actions or to specific manufacturer warranties. However, the statutes of repose applicable to design professionals generally range them as from six to 10 years. Some states, such as New York, may never terminate the exposure of the design or the selection of materials.

Consequently, if the owner or occupant cannot obtain compensation from the manufacturer, the design professional may be a target for cost recovery. Manufacturers offer only limited warranties that typically cap their liability to the replacement cost. The cost of labor, direct damages and consequential damages, such as reduced productivity, are generally excluded.

The benefits of a sustainable design often depend on how the project is commissioned, operated and maintained. Without recognition of the project owner's responsibility and a waiver of the designer's liability for the use of untested products that claim to be sustainable, the professionals liability exposure of the designer could be extreme.

Exposures to Liability

From a professional liability perspective, many exposures may be generated or intensified by any certification process or other "sustainable" calculation or promises.

Exposures include:

Unfulfilled expectations Promoting oneself as an expert without any significant experience and unique knowledge of the design principles underlying a sustainable system creates the likelihood of dissatisfied clients, who may later file claims. Therefore, certification programs such as the LEED Accredited Professional program increase professional liability exposure.

Cost recovery The broad nature of the "green" rating system can serve as a trap for design professionals attempting to design to a preselected certification level or based on product claims. Clients expect to see the financial savings that their investment is supposed to produce. Higher sustainable levels

Certification Program Costly and Outdated

City planning authorities in San Francisco offer priority permitting for construction projects registered with the U.S. Green Building Council's certification system, known as Leadership in Energy and Environmental Design, or LEED. . . .

Local developers, architects and planners credit LEED with greatly raising awareness about green building and, through its checklist of specific criteria, pushing many developers to add green features beyond what they were originally contemplating.

But the LEED certification system is not without its flaws, industry insiders said. The process can be expensive, time consuming and, perhaps most worrisome in the progressive Bay Area, out of touch with the most recent environmental building practices.

Ryan Tate,
Silicon Valley/San Jose Business Journal,
August 20, 2007.

usually require more design effort and often greater construction costs. If an anticipated benefit is not achieved—whether that benefit is lower operating costs or higher rents—the firm could be expected to pay for its "mistakes."

Implied or express warranties Certification implies energy savings and increased productivity. As the sustainability levels increase through arbitrary systems such as the LEED process, expected benefits also increase. Warranties could be claimed for anything ranging from the failure to meet the planned certification level to excessive energy, water, or maintenance costs.

If the certification states that increased daylighting and healthy indoor air quality means healthier and more productive employees, it may not matter what other factors prevent such results. Even the failure of the design to decrease employee sick leave and increase productivity "as promised" could be claimed as a breach of warranty.

Fraud or misrepresentation The savings in life-cycle costs may be misleading. If a client does not understand this, the designer could be accused of deceptive practices. Fraud or misrepresentation claims are not covered by professional liability insurance.

As with all projects, design professionals need to carefully assess the risks of sustainable designs and clients seeking such designs. Client education and client reliance on the professionalism and sound judgment of engineers and others on the design team must be promoted. Otherwise, the movement to sustainable design and the reliance on prescriptive standards that are not incorporated into building codes could result in claims against design firms.

The concept of sustainability also needs to apply to the financial viability of the design firm. Misunderstanding risks of sustainable design can result in a flow of red ink on the design firm's balance sheet.

> "Sustainable building practices can help prevent . . . claims of [sick building syndrome] by building occupants."

Eco-Architecture Can Eliminate Sick Building Syndrome

Stephen del Percio

In the following viewpoint Stephen del Percio, a New York-based lawyer and U.S. Green Building Council (USGBC) Leadership in Energy and Environmental Design (LEED) accredited professional, argues that green building practices can reduce incidences of "sick building syndrome" (SBS). He asserts that eco-architecture can reduce the business costs due to SBS-related missed work and can also limit insurance claims and lawsuits due to the syndrome. While Percio acknowledges that SBS will likely be a problem no matter how green construction practices become, many changes can be made that can improve indoor air quality and other building conditions.

As you read, consider the following questions:

1. How much electricity, oil, and gas do commercial and residential buildings use, according to Percio?

Stephen del Percio, "Green Building Practices Aim to Cure Sick Building Syndrome," *Construction Monthly*, May 8, 2007. www.constructionmonthly.com/WellSafe_01_0508 2007.html. Reproduced by permission.

2. According to a study conducted by Lawrence Berkeley National Laboratory cited by the author, how many American office workers suffer from SBS symptoms?

3. According to the EPA, as cited by Percio, how much higher can volatile organic compound materials be in indoor spaces as compared with outdoor air?

Sustainable "green" building practices can alter more than just the impact that structures have on the natural environment, although that impact is incredibly profound. The nation's commercial and residential buildings use more than sixty-two percent of our electricity, consume thirty-six percent of our oil and gas, and are responsible for thirty percent of greenhouse gas emissions. Green design principles can also help mitigate the effects that workers and residents may experience from spending substantial amounts of time inside artificial building spaces. Some of those effects can manifest themselves in what is known as sick building syndrome.

SBS Can Be Costly

Sick Building Syndrome (SBS) refers to building conditions that give rise to a variety of illnesses suffered by occupants. These conditions usually result from poor indoor air quality and include symptoms such as headaches, nausea, dizziness and fatigue. Significantly, these symptoms disappear once an occupant leaves the building. In a 1984 investigation, the World Health Organization reported that occupants in up to thirty percent of the world's new and remodeled buildings were suffering from indoor air quality–related illnesses. While SBS is typically associated with office building workers, teachers and residential dwellers have also complained of SBS ailments.

Here in the United States, a study in 2000 performed by the Lawrence Berkeley National Laboratory in California, concluded that approximately twenty-three percent of American office workers suffer from some type of SBS symptoms. Importantly, these symptoms dropped by twenty percent when air quality was improved through green design principles. The study also projected that owners stood to realize $6 billion to $14 billion in savings from reduced absenteeism owing to respiratory disease, $1 billion to $4 billion from reduced allergies and asthma, and from $20 billion to $160 billion from improved worker productivity. However, it did acknowledge that "existing data and knowledge allows only crude evidence of the magnitude of productivity gains that may be obtained by providing a cleaner indoor environments."

Most litigation resulting from allegations of SBS has involved insurance coverage. Commercial general liability policies are usually written with an absolute pollution exclusion, broadly defining the term "pollutant," and precluding insurance coverage for bodily injury or property damage arising from the discharge or release of any pollutants within a building owned or occupied by an insured. While the absolute pollution exclusion is generally effective at limiting an insurer's exposure for environmental claims, some courts have allowed claimants to challenge the language in such policies and obtain coverage in SBS scenarios.

For example, a 1997 Wisconsin case found the term "pollutant" to be ambiguous as applied to bodily injury claims. The insured was the manager of an office building that had a poorly-designed HVAC [heating, ventilation, and air-conditioning] system. Accordingly, an excessive amount of CO_2 [carbon dioxide] slowly built up throughout the office spaces. Workers contended with poor air quality resulting in headaches, nausea, and sinus problems. The insured building manager sought to obtain coverage from its insurer for the numerous claims brought by building occupants. Both the insurer and the insured had intended for the pollution exclusion clause to have broad application, but the court could not say with any degree of certainty that CO_2 should fall within the policy's definition of "pollutant." It therefore allowed the insured to obtain coverage for the claims. Sustainable building practices can help prevent not only the underlying claims of SBS by building occupants but also help to reduce the number of coverage disputes between owners and insurers.

Improving Indoor Air Quality

The USGBC's LEED green building rating system recognizes the importance of occupant health and comfort by devoting one of its five credit categories exclusively to indoor air quality. The Indoor Environmental Quality ("IEQ") credit category has two mandatory prerequisites that every project seeking any level of LEED certification must satisfy. The first, minimum indoor air quality performance, requires that the building meet the minimum requirements of ASHRAE [the American Society of Heating, Refrigerating and Air-Conditioning Engineers] 62-1999, Ventilation for Acceptable Indoor Air Quality. The second, Environmental Tobacco Smoke ("ETS") control, requires projects to either prohibit smoking entirely and locate designated exterior smoking areas at least twenty-five feet away from entries and operable windows, or provide a designated smoking area within the building which captures, contains, and removes the ETS from the building. Other credits within the IEQ category are designed to help prevent allegations of SBS and improve occupant health and comfort. Project teams can earn up to fifteen LEED credits for increased ventilation, the use of low-emitting volatile organic compound (VOC) materials (including sealants, paints, carpet systems, and woods), and provide occupants with increased daylight and personal control over thermal systems. VOCs are particularly egregious contributors to SBS because of their high vapor pressures; they can vaporize under normal atmospheric conditions into methane or benzene. The United States Environmental Protection Agency [EPA] estimates that VOCs in typical indoor spaces can be two to five

Sick Building Syndrome vs. Building Related Illness

The term "sick building syndrome" (SBS) is used to describe situations in which building occupants experience acute health and comfort effects that appear to be linked to time spent in a building, but no specific illness or cause can be identified. In contrast, the term "building related illness" (BRI) is used when symptoms of diagnosable illness are identified and can be attributed directly to airborne building contaminants.

Indicators of SBS include:

• Building occupants complain of symptoms associated with acute discomfort, e.g., headache; eye, nose, or throat irritation; dry cough; dry or itchy skin; dizziness and nausea; difficulty in concentrating; fatigue; and sensitivity to odors.

• The cause of the symptoms is not known.

• Most of the complainants report relief soon after leaving the building.

Indicators of BRI include:

• Building occupants complain of symptoms such as cough; chest tightness; fever, chills; and muscle aches

• The symptoms can be clinically defined and have clearly identifiable causes.

• Complainants may require prolonged recovery times after leaving the building.

Environmental Protection Agency,
"Indoor Air Facts No. 4 (revised)
Sick Building Syndrome," February 1991.

times greater than as those existing outdoors. At times, EPA has measured that figure at one thousand times greater.

There is currently little hard data on a consistent basis across different types of building stock from owners who have addressed indoor air quality through green design. This is in large part owing to such owners' fears of incurring liability for not having taken such measures previously. However, that has not prevented some forward-thinking owners from recognizing the importance of indoor air quality and making it an integral part of their green building projects. The Hearst Corporation's LEED Gold headquarters in Manhattan for example, uses natural ventilation during three quarters of the calendar year to bring fresh air from outside into the building. Moreover, the low-emittance coating of its exterior glass curtain wall, coupled with a paucity of interior walls, allows natural light to penetrate deep into the core of the building's office floors. Some of New York's green residential buildings also offer similar design elements. [Architectural firm] FXFOWLE's Helena [apartment building] contains low-VOC paints, gaskets to prevent smoke, odors and other pollutants from traveling between apartments, and bathroom and kitchen heat that preheats outdoor air and is sanitized by ultraviolet light prior to being supplied to the building's corridors.

While SBS will likely always be an issue no matter how green a building claims to be, the promise that new technologies and innovative designs offer in terms of mitigating the effects that buildings—both commercial and residential—have on their occupants is significant and real. Accordingly, the construction industry needs to aggressively push owners of green buildings to furnish data about performance. Doing so will encourage reluctant owners to share both successes and failures and assist construction professionals in comprehensively addressing the problems associated with SBS through sustainable design.

I "Symptom reporting appears to be due less to poor physical conditions than to poor psychosocial conditions."

Sick Building Syndrome Is Due to Job Stress Not Building Conditions

Alexi Marmot et al.

Alexi Marmot is the director of Alexi Marmot Associates, a London-based firm that conducts studies about and offers assistance to office, educational, and research organizations that have space and personnel problems. In the following viewpoint Marmot and other researchers present their findings about "sick building syndrome" (SBS). The authors' conclusions contradict most previous studies on SBS by noting that the symptoms generally associated with the syndrome are more likely tied to work-related stress than to unsafe building conditions such as poor air ventilation and airborne microbes.

As you read, consider the following questions:

1. How do the authors define "sick building syndrome"?

Alexi Marmot et al. "Building Health: An Epidemiological Study of 'Sick Building Syndrome' in the Whitehall II study," *Occupational and Environmental Medicine*, vol. 63, April 2006, pp. 283–89. Reproduced by permission.

2. Lower symptom scores were found in what kind of buildings, according to the authors?

3. According to the authors, what should managers do if SBS is reported in a building?

It has been proposed that a cluster of symptoms affecting the eyes, head, upper respiratory tract, and skin is associated with the physical properties of office buildings and costs UK businesses many millions of pounds through low productivity and sickness absence. This cluster has been labelled "sick building syndrome" (SBS). Although guidelines exist for the investigation and management of SBS, systematic research has failed to identify consistent associations between particular physical properties of buildings and SBS. There is increasing evidence that the psychosocial work environment is related to health and that the physical responses to work stress may resemble symptoms that have been attributed to the physical work environment. Work overload, lack of support at work, and conflict at work may exacerbate the effects of the physical work environment. The design of most existing studies has been such that workers report on problems with their physical work environment, levels of psychosocial work stress, and their perceived health and symptoms. Affect bias (the tendency to report consistently positively or negatively to questionnaire items because of mood) cannot be ruled out as an explanation for associations in such studies. . . .

The aim of this study is to examine whether building characteristics or psychosocial work characteristics best explain the rates of symptoms among men and women working in 44 different buildings in and around [the Whitehall area of] London. . . .

Definition of SBS

There is no single accepted definition of "sick building syndrome". The term usually refers to higher than normal prevalence in a particular building of symptoms affecting the eyes, head, upper respiratory tract, and skin. Investigation of SBS has examined office buildings in many countries including the UK, Scandinavia, and North America. Studies vary in the symptom description and frequency and whether the symptoms reduce on leaving the building.

Ten potential SBS symptoms commonly reported in other investigations were included as part of a list of 22 symptoms. Respondents were asked "Have you had any of the following symptoms in the last 14 days?". The symptoms have some validity as a health measure as they predict future sickness absence gathered from civil service records. Participants with four or more symptoms had an increased risk of sickness absence relative to those without symptoms. Psychological distress (a potential confounding factor predicting both reporting of symptoms and reporting of poor psychosocial environment), was measured by the 30-item General Health Questionnaire. . . .

Physical Environmental Characteristics of the Workstation

None of the characteristics investigated was significantly associated with symptoms. There was a suggestion that high symptom scores were associated with temperature outside the recommended range, poor relative humidity (either too damp or too dry), airborne bacteria, and the presence of inhalable dust. Unexpectedly, lower symptom scores were found in buildings with unacceptable levels of air movement, carbon dioxide, noise, airborne fungi, and volatile organic compounds, although these differences were not statistically significant.

Based on questionnaire data, workstation control was found to be inversely related to symptoms—that is, the more control people have the fewer symptoms they report.

Ventilation Systems

Overall, air conditioning was found to be associated with slightly higher symptom scores compared with other ventilation systems. Our results are consistent with previous findings, namely that fewest symptoms are associated with mechanical ventilation, followed by all air and natural ventilation, then air conditioning systems although differences across the types of ventilation system were not statistically significant. The results are clearer when the seasonal effect is removed by examining a subset of four symptoms that are constant throughout the year (headache, tired for no reason, rashes/itches and dry throat).

Psychosocial Work Characteristics

High job demands and low support at work were associated with higher mean symptom scores after adjusting for age, sex, and grade. Symptom levels tended to be higher for participants with low decision latitude although this association was not statistically significant. . . .

Psychosocial and Physical Environmental Characteristics

Those with no control over the workstation had higher symptom scores, even after adjustment for age, sex, employment grade, and other physical characteristics. Adjustments for work characteristics and GHQ [general health questionnaire] score did not substantially alter this association. These results were essentially unchanged when adjustment was made for time taken to travel to work, exposure to smoking in the workplace or in the home, and problems with housing. For participants who experienced low decision latitude, high job demands, or low support at work there was no evidence that physical environmental factors were more strongly related to symptoms than the psychosocial variables.

SBS Mislabeled

These results emphasise the potentially confounding effects of age, sex, socioeconomic position, and psychosocial aspects of work in explaining the prevalence of symptoms. They suggest that "sick building syndrome" may be wrongly named—raised symptom reporting appears to be due less to poor physical conditions than to a working environment characterised by poor psychosocial conditions. A model incorporating physical and psychosocial hazards in the work environment and health has been proposed and more recently the interplay between the indoor environment and characteristics of the building's occupants has been recognised. Control over work, job demands and work overload, job category, social stressors, mental stress at work, and personality traits have all been related to a similar set of symptoms, and a study in Africa also found that psychosocial factors were more important than physical exposures. Our findings suggest that, in this sample of office based workers, physical attributes of buildings have a small influence on symptoms.

The effects of control over the physical environment and control over work have rarely been investigated simultaneously. Our findings demonstrate that both are associated with higher symptom prevalence. Other studies suggested that the ability to control one's environment is important and our findings confirm that, even when recommended levels are achieved, employees' ability to control light levels and temperature is associated with fewer symptoms.

An important aspect of the study design was that objective measures of the physical environment were obtained by independent field workers. Many studies have obtained information on the physical office environment by questionnaire. As the same set of respondents report on perceptions of their environment and their health, this could induce spurious associations. [Our] study has the additional advantage of covering a number of buildings and a large sample of respondents who have answered a wide range of questions, including potential confounding factors. Almost every study of SBS reports that women record more symptoms than men and younger people report more symptoms than older people but not all control

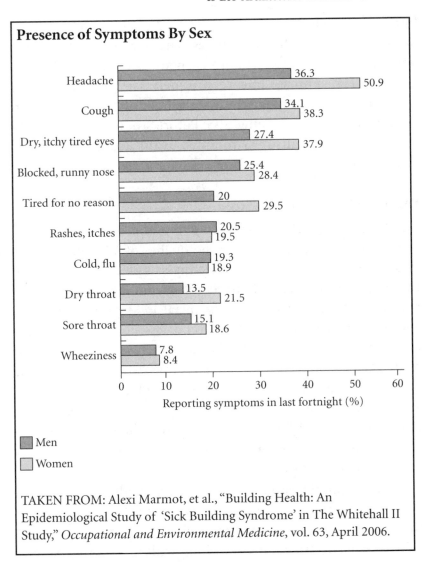

Presence of Symptoms By Sex

Symptom	Men	Women
Headache	36.3	50.9
Cough	34.1	38.3
Dry, itchy tired eyes	27.4	37.9
Blocked, runny nose	25.4	28.4
Tired for no reason	20	29.5
Rashes, itches	20.5	19.5
Cold, flu	19.3	18.9
Dry throat	13.5	21.5
Sore throat	15.1	18.6
Wheeziness	7.8	8.4

Reporting symptoms in last fortnight (%)

TAKEN FROM: Alexi Marmot, et al., "Building Health: An Epidemiological Study of 'Sick Building Syndrome' in The Whitehall II Study," *Occupational and Environmental Medicine*, vol. 63, April 2006.

for these differences. Furthermore, participants and buildings were not selected on the basis of explicit concern with sick building symptoms and responses did not arise from leading questions about whether symptoms were building related. The methods used in this paper differ from previous studies in other ways. An enquiry into questionnaires on SBS indicated that responses alter according to the list of symptoms and the format in which they are asked, and called for standard questions to be used in further studies. The phrasing of our questions on symptoms has a shorter length of recall, assisting accuracy of response. The techniques used to model the hierarchical structure of the data have not previously been used in studies investigating SBS. Future studies of SBS should ask for recent recall of symptoms, avoid leading questions, and adjust for age, sex, and socioeconomic position.

Important Considerations

The lack of association between symptoms and the physical environment could be because the quality of Whitehall buildings is above a threshold for affecting symptoms. If this is the case then claims that SBS affects most buildings and most office workers and causes great financial losses are unfounded, and the search for the cause of SBS is less important in terms of public health. If it is not the case, then it is important to study typical conditions in places representative of most office buildings. This study contains a sample of buildings selected as housing people already participating in a health study rather than ones where SBS was suspected and is therefore more useful in studying the public health implications of the physical environment at work. . . .

These findings should not be interpreted as justification for assuming that the quality of the physical environment of the workplace is unimportant. Comfort and perceived satisfaction with environmental conditions within buildings should not be ignored. Compared to current standards, the results showed that some features are generally acceptable (carbon dioxide, lighting levels, and noise) but that many workstations were too hot, with too little air movement. These conditions can and should be improved even if health outcomes are unchanged.

In this study, the physical environment of workstations and office buildings appears to have less effect on symptom prevalence than features of the psychosocial environment. SBS symptoms are more about the jobs people do, their psychosocial environment, and their ability to control conditions in their office than about the physical environment of the building or workstation where the job is performed. The results imply that if SBS is reported in a building, management should consider causes beyond the physical design and operation of the workplace and should widen their investigation to include the organisation of work roles and the autonomy of the workforce.

Periodical Bibliography

The following articles have been selected to supplement the diverse views presented in this chapter.

Raluca Albu	"Smart Towns," *On Earth*, Summer 2007.
Lois Arkin	"An Urban Ecovillage of the Near Future," *Communities*, December 2005.
Design News	"Businesses Gain Interest in Sustainable Buildings," June 25, 2007.
Alex Frangos	"Will Insulating with Straw Catch Fire?" *Wall Street Journal*, August 9, 2006.
Jeff Nachtigal	"It's Easy and Cheap Being Green," *Fortune*, October 16, 2006.
New York Times Magazine	"The New Green Building," May 20, 2007.
Neal Peirce	"'Green' Sounds Great—but Is It Affordable?" *Nation's Cities Weekly*, July 12, 2004.
Robert Ries et al.	"The Economic Benefits of Green Buildings: A Comprehensive Case Study," *Engineering Economist*, vol. 51 no. 3, 2006.
Angela Spivey	"Going Green Saves over Time," *Environmental Health Perspectives*, April 2004.
Janice Tuchman	"Big Owners Balance Triple Bottom Line," *ENR: Engineering NewsRecord*, August 9, 2004.
Cheryl Weber	"The Green House Effect: Eco-friendly Design Grows More Practical and More Acceptable," *Residential Architect*, March 1, 2005.
Jonathan C. Weiss, Kath Williams, and Judith Heerwagen	"How to Design for Humans," *Architecture*, April 2004.
Alex Wilson	"What Is Green Building?" *Mother Earth News*, August/September 2005.

OPPOSING
VIEWPOINTS®
SERIES

CHAPTER 2

How Does Eco-Architecture Impact the Environment?

Chapter Preface

As open land becomes more scarce and concerns about the environment intensify, city planners and residents are coming together to find ways of making the most of urban landscapes. Many state and city governments have turned to transit villages, which centralize businesses and residences around public transportation systems, as a means of curbing the impact humans have on the environment, encouraging business growth, and bringing people together. Although transit villages are not utopias and can suffer from the same types of problems as other planned communities, experts argue that they offer an alternative to unplanned urban sprawl and can lead to the revitalization of downtown areas that have long been abandoned for the suburbs.

Michael Bernick and Robert Cervero describe the main characteristics of transit villages in their book *Transit Villages in the 21st Century*. According to the authors, transit stations must be at the heart of these smart communities. Residents and nonresidents must be able to reach the station within about a five-minute walk and all other areas around the station must be devoted to encouraging community togetherness. Since 1999, New Jersey has established nineteen transit villages that are located within a mile radius of train stations. Although it could take decades to determine whether these sites are successful in terms of their intended purpose, the popularity of transit villages among businesses and potential residents has encouraged the state to devote billions of dollars to new and continuing development.

Not everyone supports transit villages, however. Critics argue that they can create more problems than they fix, such as increased traffic and lack of parking due to nonresidents patronizing community businesses. Others wonder if the environmental impact of more residents using public transportation will be enough to combat the often enormous scale of transit villages. For example, construction is underway for three transit villages in Los Angeles, which include six sky-scrapers, twenty-nine hundred new homes, and vast shopping and entertainment centers. Perhaps the most difficult hurdle that smart communities must overcome is changing the way residents think. Just because the train is available does not guarantee that it will be used. In regard to the Los Angeles developments, *Los Angeles Times* writer Cara Mia DiMassa wonders, "The question is whether the people who move into the three new developments are willing to alter their lifestyles accordingly."

Although some critics of transit villages, such as Michael Park, argue that they promote "a sentimental view of the 'old country' and the 'good ole days' and [force] it on modern society," many Americans are at least receptive to the idea of communities centralized around high-quality transportation systems. Like the authors in this chapter, they too wonder if smart communities and other eco-friendly projects will actually improve the quality of life on Earth. As with other quests for radical social change, only time will reveal which plans yield the most benefits.

| "Buildings are the worst thing that people do to the environment."

Eco-Architecture Will Help the Environment

Jeffrey Kaye

In the following viewpoint Jeffrey Kaye, a reporter for KCET, the Public Broadcasting Service affiliate in Los Angeles, interviews a number of green building supporters. The interviewees argue that commercial and residential buildings have a negative impact on the environment that can be at least partially remedied by employing green building practices. Environmental activists, architects, and home owners are beginning to see the value of eco-architecture in saving the environment. Although some designers and contractors still resist green building initiatives, the interviewees argue that the benefits outweigh the costs and the additional education needed to make architecture more sustainable.

As you read, consider the following questions:

1. What percentage of electricity in the United States is consumed by homes and office buildings, according to Rob Watson?

Jeffrey Kaye, "Eco-Friendly Buildings," *Online NewsHour (PBS)*, April 15, 2005. Reproduced by permission.

2. According to a study done by the state of California, as cited by Kaye, how much does 2 percent in additional cost in a green building's design save in energy costs over the life of the building?

3. What two green building features will the proposed Freedom Tower have when it is completed, according to Kaye?

Jeffrey Kaye: Think about what harms the environment and the culprits that most likely come to mind are factories, power plants and cars, all belching pollutants. What probably isn't thought of as an environmental menace are America's more than 80 million commercial and residential buildings.

But whether they're soaring skyscrapers or suburban tract homes, buildings have a huge effect on the environment, say scientists, from the consumption of energy and the wasteful use of raw materials to the production of greenhouse gases.

Rob Watson: Well, I believe that buildings are the worst thing that people do to the environment.

Kaye: Rob Watson is a senior scientist with the environmental group NRDC, The Natural Resources Defense Council.

Watson: Buildings use twice as much energy as cars and trucks. Seventy percent of the electricity in the United States is consumed by our homes and our office buildings.

Kaye: Because of their high energy consumption, buildings are indirectly responsible for air pollution, a third of the country's total carbon dioxide emissions and half of its sulfur dioxide emissions.

Watson: We don't associate the fact that when we turn on a light switch, coal is mined in a mine; it goes to a power plant that comes up the stack as acid rain–producing sulfur dioxide, planet-cooking carbon dioxide. There's no direct connection between the environmental impact that the building causes and the damage is always somewhere else.

Green Building Works

Kaye: In response to growing awareness of the building environment's effect on the natural environment, architects and builders, activists and government agencies are increasingly championing an alternative method of design and construction. It's an approach called green building.

The essence of green building is creating structures that are far more efficient in their consumption of energy and water, and less wasteful in their use of materials than conventional buildings. Once a movement on the architectural fringe, green design principles are starting to appear in everything from a new generation of government buildings and corporate offices to single family homes and apartment complexes.

This place, the NRDC's West Coast office in Santa Monica, California, is considered the greenest building in America, according to the U.S. Green Building Council, an organization that rates buildings according to their energy efficiency and environmental quality.

Opened in the fall of 2003, the 15,000-square-foot structure consumes 70 percent less energy than a non-green building of equivalent size and function. Solar panels on the roof generate 20 percent of the building's electricity. Toilets use a gallon less water per flush than conventional ones. The floors are made of easily replenished woods like bamboo and poplar. Ample skylights direct sunshine deep into the building and reduce reliance on electrical lighting.

Watson: And all of these combine to make a more comfortable, more effective to operate, and yet highly cost-effective space.

Kaye: Watson is especially fond of showing off the building's state-of-the-art water recycling plant in the basement.

Watson: The biology is killed with ozone here.

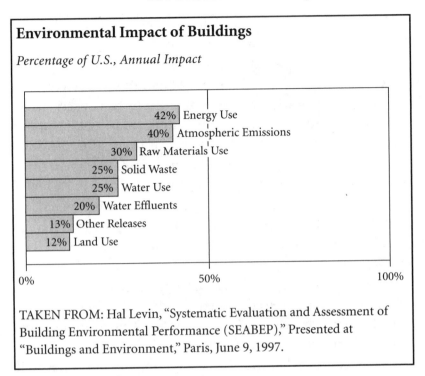

Environmental Impact of Buildings

Percentage of U.S., Annual Impact

- 42% Energy Use
- 40% Atmospheric Emissions
- 30% Raw Materials Use
- 25% Solid Waste
- 25% Water Use
- 20% Water Effluents
- 13% Other Releases
- 12% Land Use

0%   50%   100%

TAKEN FROM: Hal Levin, "Systematic Evaluation and Assessment of Building Environmental Performance (SEABEP)," Presented at "Buildings and Environment," Paris, June 9, 1997.

Kaye: It cleans the building's gray water—that's the water that comes from the sinks in the bathroom and kitchen, as well as from captured rainwater.

Watson: It's purified a number of times and disinfected a number of times, reverse osmosis. It's better than bottled water. It's better than tap water. I drink it all the time.

Architects Embrace Green Building

Kaye: Environmental groups are not the only ones embracing green design.

Dan Heinfeld: We think it's a fabulous design tool, that green architecture really lends itself to some very interesting architectural practices.

Kaye: Dan Heinfeld is president of LPA, an architectural firm in Irvine, California, which specializes in green building design.

Heinfeld: So we'll get the light without the heat gain and that will be a good, sustainable practice.

I'm now dealing with my clients about energy use, the indoor environment that their employees and users are going to have, and just how they sort of work within this space. And I think those are much more tangible things to be talking about in creating great architecture than sort of decorating the box.

Kaye: Heinfeld's firm designed a green building for a company better known for its fuel-efficient cars. Toyota's 624,000-square-foot sales office in Torrance, California, is a green giant. In fact, it's the largest green building complex in America. Its roof, carpeted in solar panels, generates enough electricity to power 500 homes.

The building uses reclaimed water for landscaping and for cooling. And the material used to make the office complex comes largely from recycled automobiles. That includes steel in the building itself and lobby furniture made from old seatbelts. Heinfeld says that the Toyota Building demonstrates that green building principles are no longer experimental or avante garde.

Heinfeld: We think those are the really powerful examples because it shows that it really can be done mainstream and it can be done on any kind of project.

Support for Green Building

Kaye: A further encouragement for green building projects has come from cities, states and government agencies, which in recent years have enacted green building standards. The city of Santa Monica was one of the first communities in the country to put green construction codes on the books.

Dean Kubani, who oversees Santa Monica's environmental programs, says the city was motivated as much by dollars and cents concerns as by environmental ones.

Dean Kubani: If you just look at green building, if you make a building more energy efficient and water efficient, it's going to save you money over the long run. And we here in the city, we own a lot of buildings and private developers own a lot of buildings here, and if they can save money over the 50-year life span of those buildings, it makes sense to do it.

Kaye: Green building can often cost more than conventional construction. Solar panels and water purification systems, for instance, will increase builders' budgets. But proponents say higher up-front costs will pay for themselves in the long run.

A recent State of California study reported that 2 percent additional cost in a green building's design translates into savings of up to 20 percent in energy costs over the life span of the building.

In Santa Monica, green buildings range from the police headquarters, to a low-income housing project, which generates much of its power from solar energy. The city, in cooperation with the environmental group Global Green, has also opened up a green building resource center. In it, homeowners can get information about a smorgasbord of green building products. . . .

Resistance to Green Building

Kaye: Despite its growth, green building still meets resistance, often from designers and contractors who are uncomfortable with changing their ways and are unfamiliar with green building practices and materials. . . .

Kaye: That's been a frustration for Daniel McGee and Catherine Lerer, who have been coming to the center for nearly a year as they remodel their house.

Daniel McGee: I was probably struck by how in general the people we talk to, particularly architects and contractors, know so little about this and what's available and the things that we can do. So part of the process has been trying to educate our architect and contractors to open up their eyes a little bit, that a lot of the traditional materials they use, there are alternatives to them.

Kaye: Looking ahead, the highest profile green building project in America promises to be Freedom Tower, which is to be built on the former World Trade Center site in New York. When finished, the more than 1,700-foot-tall structure will include massive solar panels and its own wind farm on the upper floors.

> *"Green building is a good idea ... but don't fool yourself that it is going to save the planet."*

Eco-Architecture's Benefits to the Environment Are Exaggerated

Jane Powell

Jane Powell is a renovator of old homes and the author of a number of architectural design books, including Bungalow Details: Interior. *In the following viewpoint she argues that green building is simply a fad whose benefits to the environment have been overstated. After all, she asserts, building and remodeling use resources no matter if they have been recycled or salvaged. Also, supposedly eco-friendly products, like multi-glazed window sashes and fluorescent light bulbs, may actually harm the environment. While it is better for the environment to take some steps towards sustainable building practices, these efforts will not save the Earth.*

Jane Powell, "Green Envy: What are the true environmental benefits of the 'green' house movement?," *San Francisco Chronicle*, May 13, 2007. Reproduced by permission of the author.

As you read, consider the following questions:

1. According to Donovan Rypkema, as cited by Powell, demolishing ten thousand square feet of old buildings cancels out the environmental impact of recycling how many aluminum cans?

2. What is the average life span of a double-glazed window unit, according to the author?

3. What does Powell say was the square footage of the average-size house in 1970?

"Green building" is the feel-good trend of the moment. Cities stipulate it, builders market it and home buyers supposedly demand it. Who could be against it? It's the panacea that will combat global warming, prevent sprawl, revitalize our downtowns, contribute to the region's economic growth and keep California on the leading edge. So everyone is embracing green building as if they were French kissing George Clooney. It always sounds easy—you just get some low-VOC [volatile organic compounds] paint, some linoleum, some wheatboard cabinets, make your garden gate out of cast-off Volvo parts, and presto!—greenness is achieved without any serious thinking about the real effects of your choices on the planet. The reality is far more complicated. The "easy" choices are a cop-out—not that you shouldn't do them—but they won't balance out that SUV you're driving.

Green Building Is an Oxymoron

Building or remodeling uses up resources, even if those resources are recycled or salvaged. The greenest thing you can do is continue the life of an existing building, whose resources have already been extracted. Retrofitting an existing building for better energy efficiency, lower water use and so forth is greener than building new.

There is an all-too-common practice of demolishing a small existing building in order to throw up (I use the term deliberately) a larger "green" building, as though the small building had volunteered to be the virgin (timber) sacrifice on the altar of "smart growth." Often it is promised that materials from the building will be reused, but I guarantee there is one thing that never gets re-used: lath [narrow strips of wood nailed across wall studs]. A small pre-World War II house contains several thousand linear feet of lath, all sawn from old-growth timber, which, even if recycled, will simply end up as mulch. We dutifully recycle our aluminum cans, yet demolishing 10,000 square feet of old buildings wipes out the environmental benefit of recycling 2,688,000 aluminum cans, according to figures compiled by Donovan Rypkema of Place Economics in Washington, D.C. We are also assured that these "green" replacement buildings will prevent farmland from being paved in the Central Valley, though really the only connection between these two things is a different kind of green—the kind with dead presidents on it. Erecting a green building in the city will not prevent even 1 square foot of farmland from being developed as long as there is money to be made in doing so.

Fluorescent vs. Incandescent Bulbs

For the past umpteen years various people and organizations have tried to browbeat us into using compact fluorescent bulbs (CFLs). People have been remarkably resistant to doing so. So [California] Assemblyman Lloyd Levine (D-Van Nuys), Chair of the Utilities and Commerce Committee, is attempting to legislate a ban on incandescent bulbs by 2012. We already have Title 24, a piece of legislation that mandates hard-wired fluorescents in kitchens and bathrooms, among other things. The push for fluorescents ignores the fact that greater energy savings could be achieved through better wall and ceiling insulation, or low-interest loans or grants for solar power. It's not the incandescents that pollute (unlike CFLs, which contain mercury and can only be recycled at hazardous waste collection centers, not that anybody bothers . . .), but it's the production of electricity used to power them that's the issue. However, addressing that end of the problem doesn't lend itself to a sound bite.

One notes there is no talk of banning SUVs, wide-screen TVs or whirlpool tubs. CFLs are all produced in China, where wages and environmental standards are lower. Although the EPA [Environmental Protection Agency] (energystar.gov) says CFLs last 10 times longer than incandescents (about seven years), they admit the average life is more like five years, which means some don't even last that long. Lamp life, according to General Electric, is defined as the point when 50 percent of the bulbs in a statistically large sample have died. Under laboratory conditions, half of the CFLs will have gone out at 10,000 hours (six hours per day equals 4.56 years). In less-than-ideal conditions in a house, they will often die sooner—in enclosed fixtures or humid bathrooms because the heat- and moisture-sensitive ballasts will fail prematurely, or in places where they are switched on and off a lot. LEDs [light emitting diodes] may be the answer, but they aren't widely available, and at the current price of $50 for an LED with a standard Edison base, I don't think many people will be rushing out to buy them.

Modern Replacement Windows

No discussion of green building comes without a recommendation for using double- or triple-glazed window sashes, even though that will only create a minor increase in its insulation rating (as opposed to a major increase for an insulated 2-by-4 wall). PG&E [Pacific Gas and Electric Company] will happily give you a rebate to replace your single-glazed windows with new double-glazed ones, ignoring the fact that the average life span of a double-glazing unit is only 10 years (some companies now offer a 20-year guarantee), or that a single-glazed window can be equally energy-efficient with the addi-

Deep Green Building

The very last step of deep green building would be utilizing the many types of eco-stuff that have been introduced in recent years. Just a few of what are available include heating/cooling systems that use 50% less energy; geothermal systems that utilize temperatures beneath a home; insulating glass; solar panels; solatubes that can provide light to basements from the second floor; and earth building with natural materials or salvage materials.

The problem is when the eco-gadget tail wags the urban dog. Thinking of green homes as nothing but a sum of eco-gadgets leads to viewing cities as nothing but a sum of eco-homes. The inability to design green neighborhoods means eco-homes actually help perpetuate urban sprawl. . . .

Building practices that ain't green have a gadget fetish that is blind to the big picture. Deep green building would focus on low-tech and no-tech solutions. Deep green building would integrate transportation into home design. Deep green building would aim to improve living space while decreasing the gross domestic product, a concept which is anathema to shallow green economics.

Don Fitz, Z Magazine, July 6, 2007.

tion of a storm window, according to a study conducted by the Oak Ridge National Laboratory.

How green is it to replace your windows every 10 or 20 years? Even the U.S. Green Building Council realizes that replacing single-glazed windows in existing buildings makes no sense, saying, "taking a window from R-1 to R-3 (insulation rating) will not provide sufficient energy savings to offset the cost of replacement windows and associated waste. Historic windows were constructed of dense old growth wood. The life cycle of modern replacement windows is much shorter." Millions of wooden windows are sent to landfills every year, and the few that aren't are languishing at the local salvage yard. New wood windows use fast-growing lumber, which is less durable. Worse, many new or replacement windows are vinyl (PVC). Vinyl is a petroleum product and toxic chemicals are used in manufacturing it. PVC resin is useless on its own and requires stabilizers made from heavy metals in order to be used for windows. Vinyl is also ubiquitous, therefore difficult to avoid—your shower curtain, your electrical wiring, the dashboard of your hybrid car—all vinyl.

Size Does Matter

In 1970, the average house was 1,500 square feet. Nationally, it's now 2,200, and in the [San Francisco] Bay Area, new houses average closer to 3,000 square feet. Ted Turner's daughter, Laura Turner Seydel, recently completed a 6,000-square-foot "Eco-Manor" in Atlanta. I suppose it's better that rich people build green, but according to *Fortune* magazine, her husband is currently lobbying the U.S. Green Building Council [USGBC] to ease their restrictions for LEED (Leadership in Energy and Environmental Design) certification, because the USGBC favors small homes, which effectively penalizes the rich and their need to live large. Cue the violins. Do they want points for not building a 12,000-square-foot house?

None of us are free of environmental sin. I own a historic 3,800-square-foot house containing an obscene amount of old growth timber. I can't bring those trees back—all I can do is lessen the building's environmental footprint as best I can, with more insulation, storm windows, a more efficient furnace. In this, like most of us, I get no financial help. The "Eco-Manor" cost $1.5 million—most of us are not in that income bracket. We do what we can—turn down our thermostats, try to recycle, drive less. We do that because we feel powerless against the real issues: overpopulation, a government that protects corporate profits, an economy based on continually escalating consumption. On some level we are aware that if things were different we would already be driving electric cars that recharge through photovoltaic cells on the roof, free solar power would have been provided on a huge scale, along with free insulation for every building lacking it. Instead of spending billions on the war in Iraq, we would be using those billions to provide birth control and education for women worldwide. Green building is a good idea, certainly if you're going to build or remodel, try to be as green as possible—but don't fool yourself that it's going to save the planet.

"The couple's home may be considered large by some green building proponents ... But [Elise] adds, one of their intentions was to inspire ordinary folks who aren't necessarily concerned about building a home that is gentler to the Earth."

Large Houses Can Be Eco-Friendly

Claire Anderson

In the following viewpoint, Claire Anderson examines the construction of a 2,400-square-foot straw bale house by Elise Lang and Michael Pierce in rural Georgia, arguing that straw bale construction can combine architectural style with minimal environmental impact. The benefits of straw bale are enhanced by the use of additional eco-friendly fixtures such as salvaged materials, energy-efficient appliances, natural light and ventilation. Claire Anderson is a member of the editorial staff at Mother Earth News in which the following viewpoint appeared.

As you read, consider the following questions:

1. What is the insulative value of straw bale vs. typical wood-framed construction?
2. What was one of the goals for Elise in deciding to build a straw bale home?
3. How were salvaged materials employed in the construction?

Near the end of a dirt road that weaves in and out of the woods outside Farmington, Ga., sits a tasteful Southern farmhouse owned by Elise Lang and Michael Pierce. Its wide hip roof and the deep eaves that cover the wraparound porch echo the era of mint juleps, seersucker suits and the sweet twang of banjos.

But look a little closer and you'll find a house that puts a new twist on tradition—the "truth window," a small 6-by-6-inch hole on the north wall of the foyer, says it all: This house is built with straw bales.

Standing in the home's entryway, with its tall ceilings rising to a 20-foot peak and dramatic arched passageways to the home's interior, you can easily overlook the truth window. At first, the unplastered patch seems like an imperfection in this nearly new home, but it reveals what makes Elise and Michael's house so distinctive: This house is a straw bale structure—the first permitted in Oconee County, Ga., according to officials there, and according to the couple, perhaps the first in the state.

Dixie Meets Determination

Elise, a former U.S. Army captain, stumbled across straw bale building while stationed at Fort Huachuca, Ariz. "I was looking for a place to live, and some people told me about Mary Diamond, who was looking for someone to take care of her straw bale home," Elise says. Although she couldn't leave her post to be a caretaker, Elise took the opportunity to tour

Mary's house. The home's amazing insulative qualities appealed to her environmental sensibilities, but Elise distinctly recalls that it was the feeling of the house—the sense that you were embraced, snug and cozy inside the structure—that captured her heart.

"It was the sense of being connected to nature, and the feeling of peace and harmony that inspired me," Elise says. "It's the same feeling I get when I'm in the woods or the mountains; the Earth connection, except it was inside this amazing home."

Homecoming

Fourteen years ago, at the urging of friends, Elise purchased 50 wooded acres with a 650-square-foot passive-solar cabin outside of Athens, home of her alma mater, the University of Georgia. She visited the property when she could but decided that because she was stationed across the country, she needed a caretaker.

Enter Michael Pierce: artist, world traveler and self-proclaimed Supreme Bean (he started what may have been the first tofu processing plant in Germany in the 1980s). In 1991, after returning to his native Georgia from travels in Europe and India, Michael took the caretaking job, living in the little cabin and maintaining the land for Elise. He finally met his landlord three years later, and sparks flew. They maintained a long-distance relationship for several months, until he joined her in Arizona. But Dixie kept calling the native Southerners home—Elise originally hails from New Orleans; Michael's family lives in Macon, Ga. The next year, Elise resigned her Army commission, and the couple settled into the cabin on the Georgia property.

Although the 1970s earth-sheltered cabin met immediate needs for housing, Elise still dreamed of building a straw bale home and turning the old cabin into an art studio for Michael.

She began to read everything on straw bale building she could find, starting with what she says is "the bible of straw bale building"—The Straw Bale House by Athena and Bill Steen ... During a 1995 trip to Europe, she toted along this tome, dog-earing page after page and making notes in the margins. When she and Michael returned to the United States, she says, "I made the dozens of phone calls that I was dying to make [while we were] overseas. I had lots of questions that I wanted answered."

Elise's primary concern was the humid climate of northeastern Georgia. All of her readings described homes built in arid climates, and she doubted that straw bale could stay dry in the sultry South. "I decided to call The Last Straw [a straw bale building periodical] to subscribe," she says. "Joanne De Havillan answered, and we started talking about straw bale building. I told her that I'd really like to do it, but my property was in Georgia." And then she said, "Don't you know about the 68-year-old straw bale mansion in Alabama?"—The home De Havillan referred to was the Burritt Museum in Huntsville, a large two-story straw bale house, built in 1936 and still standing strong after almost seven decades. "From that point on," Elise says, "I was encouraged that a straw bale house was possible in the South."

Blending Beauty and Efficiency

From then on, during her commutes to and from work, Elise took mental notes on the homes she passed en route. She says she always has admired the clean, solid lines of hip roofs and the charm of wraparound porches, typical of the South. So when it came time to design her own home, Elise wanted it to reflect such Southern building traditions. "I wanted the house to appeal to a wide audience—to inspire even conventional families to build with straw bales," she says. "I wanted to impress the typically conservative-minded bankers, home appraisers, insurance agents and building inspectors. I wanted this home to give straw bale a good reputation here in the South, and I wanted to present a house that would balance beauty and efficiency."

But she and Michael needed some help to create the home that existed in Elise's mind's eye. They found it in architect Howard Switzer of Linden, Tenn.

Down to Earth Design

Switzer belies the typical architect. First, there's his appearance: he bears an uncanny resemblance to Jerry Garcia, the late Grateful Dead singer and guitarist. Then, there's his history: Fresh out of high school, Switzer started work as a draftsman in an Illinois architectural firm. He eventually moved to Tennessee, where he took the architectural exams and passed all nine on his first attempt.

For 10 years, he lived at The Farm, a famed intentional community on the outskirts of Summertown, Tenn. . . . As an architect, Switzer immediately recognized the merits of using straw bales as a building material. Since his start with straw bale construction, he and [his wife, Katey] Culver have consulted on and designed two to three straw bale homes each year. Elise and Michael met him at a weekend straw bale workshop at The Farm, and . . . hired him to design their home.

"Elise sent me photos of houses in the area she liked," Switzer says, "and we worked up a design that incorporated those traditional elements, like high ceilings and tall doors. The plan was an organic process that came out of Elise and Michael's needs."

Setting The Precedent

After the plans were drawn, changed and drawn again, Elise presented them to the Oconee County, Ga., authorities to obtain a building permit. She also gave them copies of approved straw bale construction codes from other states, as well as the names and phone numbers of code officials who had worked with straw bale construction. In addition, she provided videos of fire tests done on straw bale walls and a page from The Last Straw that addressed common concerns about straw bale construction.

"I wanted to share my knowledge with them, because that's what The Last Straw taught me to do: Be prepared to educate, rather than alienate, building code officials," Elise says.

William White, former Oconee County code enforcement director, approved the couple's building permit—it was the first for a straw bale house in that county. "Under the Southern Building Code, which we followed at the time Elise and Michael's house was being built, there's nothing that said you couldn't build [a non-load-bearing straw bale home]," White says. "The design of the house was structurally sound, and everything other than the straw complied with the codes. And there was nothing that expressly forbade using straw in your walls, either."

Moving from Inspiration to Perspiration

The couple decided to be their own contractor, but Michael was visiting friends in Europe when Elise broke ground in August 1999. "I came home to a huge muddy hole in the ground," Michael says.

Although he recalls having some anxiety about acting as the contractor, Elise says she wasn't worried. "I knew I needed a master carpenter who could say the structural systems, the foundation and the post-and-beams were sound," she says. "I felt we had enough knowledge of straw bale that we could make a good, solid home with the right carpenter." And, true to her persistent nature, Elise found the right person, Bill Perry, a master carpenter who lived just down the road.

Elise and Michael also hired others to help with construction, including Doug Cashman, a friend from Taos, N.M., who helped with the framing and plastering. Masons set the concrete block for the 826-square-foot basement, and Michael followed them, filling all the blocks with rebar and concrete. He originally lugged cement to the blocks in a 5-gallon bucket, but "finally wised-up" and hired a concrete pump truck. "It was the best $300 I ever spent," he says.

Construction progressed quickly. The basement floor was finished in a week, and the framing work got under way the following week. Door and window headers were milled from yellow pine harvested on site.

Massive roof trusses—45 feet long—were manufactured off site, trucked in and placed by crane. Elise was astonished at the amount of wood they used in their straw bale house. "I couldn't believe it," she says. "Here I was building this straw bale house, thinking that I was saving wood, and then the trusses arrived. In retrospect, I would have designed a simpler roof that required less wood to build."

The roof sheeting—galvanized metal roofing screwed to purlins—was completed by mid-October.

If You Build It, They Will Come

Elise and Michael found straw bales through their local county extension agent. They timed the cutting to reap the driest harvest, and Michael arranged to temporarily store the bales in a friend's chicken house. "It's crucial to store them properly," Elise says. "People out West don't have to worry about it so much. But that's the secret to straw bale—get the straw dry and keep it dry."

The home's first straw-bale wall raising occurred two weeks before Christmas. Switzer and Culver facilitated the raising and Elise, Michael and a slew of their friends provided labor. Elise says she spent much of her time teaching new recruits the finer points of stacking straw bales, tying off half-bales and squaring up corners. Both she and Michael say they enjoyed the community-building aspect of straw bale building, although they also admit that it wasn't as efficient as an organized workshop where everyone is on the same schedule.

"We'd just finish having a mini-lecture on tying bales, and a whole new batch of folks would arrive, and I'd have to start over and orient them to the process," Elise says. "But despite the discontinuity in people, we still managed to get almost all the bales stacked in three days."

For stability and to keep the bale walls plumb, long pieces of bamboo were fastened to both sides of the walls. At regular intervals, a stitch of polypropylene twine runs through the walls, cinching the bamboo to the bales like a corset. Now covered with three coats of plaster, the bamboo is barely perceptible.

Native Red Clay Plaster

Red Georgia clay lends warmth to the home's natural lime plaster walls. After experimenting with different plaster recipes, Elise called Switzer for advice.—"'Remember that recipe I gave you?' he reminded me," Elise says.—'It's 2,000 years old. I think it'll work.'—The semipermeable coating sheds water while allowing the straw bale walls to breathe, a crucial component of building with bales.

The clay-lime plaster was mixed on site and applied by hand and trowel; coating the interior and exterior with three layers of plaster was a time-consuming process that took several plastering parties. Michael completed much of the painstaking plastering work himself over several months, finishing the work in mid-March 2002. The sculptor in him craved experimenting with the material, to give the walls an organic feel and texture, and his artist's touch is evident throughout the home. The ripple of curves at the northwest corner of the guest bedroom, the niches carved out to fit a contemplative clay figure ... and the long ribs of bamboo that rise subtly from the east living room wall are examples of his work.

Finishing Touches

Michael and Elise are unabashed gleaners; their expert eyes have spotted many treasures at flea markets, estate sales and

The First EcoMansion

From the outside, the Seydel family's new home looks like any old Tudor manse. But who would guess that this is the largest eco-friendly house in America? With its 27 photovoltaic panels on the roof, solar tubes that snake into interior rooms, geothermal heat pumps, and rainwater-collecting cisterns, this is, in fact, the first home over 5,000 square feet ever to be certified by the U.S. Green Building Council—and evidence of a new wave of eco-building that doesn't look like eco-building. . . .

[Laura Turner Seydel] and her husband, Rutherford, an environmental lawyer, spent $1.5 million to construct Eco-Manor—some 10 percent extra for going green.

Patricia Sellers, Fortune, *March 19, 2007.*

salvage yards. Their home's glowing hardwood floors were milled from 100-year-old heart of pine beams salvaged from an old Athens, Ga., warehouse. Reclaimed bead board, harvested from a Macon, Ga., warehouse, lends rustic character to the great room's interior walls. The guest bathroom's floors, walls and shower are finished with slate roofing tiles reclaimed from a friend's scrap pile.

The dramatic walnut closet doors that stretch almost to the master bedroom's ceiling once served as pocket doors in a Georgia plantation home. Cleverly concealed behind another set of doors is an Energy Star Frigidaire Gallery series horizontal-axis washer and a Frigidaire high-efficiency dryer.

At 2,400 square feet, the couple's home may be considered large by some green building proponents; even Elise offers some gracious apologies. But, she adds, one of their intentions was to inspire ordinary folks who aren't necessarily concerned about building a home that is gentler to the Earth. "We wanted to balance beauty and efficiency and show people that you can bring these concepts together in a natural and harmonious way," Elise says.

The home performs exceptionally well during the sweltering Southern summers. A small air conditioner is rarely used, and then only to help wring the humidity out of the living space. The home's high ceilings, ceiling fans, and large doors and windows help keep fresh air circulating throughout the house. The basement, which maintains moderate temperatures year-round, and a fan in the attic to purge hot air, also help the house keep its cool.

The home's thick straw bale walls provide an insulative value about twice as good as a typical wood-framed stud wall insulated with fiberglass batts. Large, south-facing glass doors admit an abundance of sunlight during the winter months to help warm the house, and lighting a fire in the woodstove thwarts the chill. Argon gas-filled, double-pane Anderson doors and windows also contribute to the the home's energy efficiency.

Michael and Elise use propane for their cooking, hot water and backup space heating needs. Their Vestrost Eco-Fridge (also called ConServ) refrigerator requires only 330 kilowatt-hours of electricity per year to operate. (Even Energy Star-rated refrigerators of the same size consume about 10 percent more electricity than this highly efficient model.) An Energy Star Bosch stainless steel dishwasher blends with custom kitchen cabinets.

Natural light washes over almost every room in the house, except for the guest bathroom, which lies within four interior walls. But even there, light seeps in through a small, half-moon sidelight. And all but one room has outdoor access. French doors in the dining room, living room and master bedroom open onto the wraparound deck. The master bath and guest room both access a screened-in porch area on the west side of the house—a haven from gnats and mosquitoes that plague Southern summer evenings.

Setting a Standard

"We set out to build an exemplary straw bale home, one that could set a standard for alternative building in this area," Elise says. . . . During the past two years, Elise and Michael have continued to monitor their home's performance—even going so far as to drill a few small holes in the walls to check for moisture. To date, even the east-facing exterior wall that receives the brunt of the stormy weather remains bone dry.

"We wanted to be so exemplary," Elise says, "so other code officials can come out here and touch the walls, feel the plaster, and understand that straw bale buildings can be successful, even in the South."

> *"For a given house design ... the bigger its square footage, the bigger its environmental footprint."*

Large Houses Cannot Be Eco-Friendly

Stan Cox

In the following viewpoint Stan Cox, a plant breeder and nature writer, argues that although some home builders and home owners believe that their building practices and materials are green, the sheer size of these new homes prohibits them from such a designation. He asserts that more Americans want bigger houses even though family size has decreased in the past several decades. Unfortunately, Cox notes, only a small number of new houses are as energy efficient as they could be, which makes large houses even harder on the environment.

As you read, consider the following questions:

1. How much carbon dioxide does the transportation of concrete to build a typical 2,500-square-foot house generate, according to Cox?

2. How much more wood, according to the author, can a "green"-built house use in comparison to a standard-built house of the same size?

Stan Cox, "Big Houses Are Not Green: America's McMansion Problem," *AlterNet*, October 21, 2007. www.alternet.org/story/61523/. Reproduced by permission.

3. How much can a typical house designed to LEED specifications expect to save in energy over twenty years, according to Cox?

The National Association of Home Builders (NAHB) estimates that 42 percent of newly built houses now have more than 2,400 square feet of floorspace, compared with only 10 percent in 1970. In 1970 there were so few three-bathroom houses that they didn't even show up in NAHB statistics. By 2005, one out of every four new houses had at least three bathrooms.

Smaller families are living in bigger houses. In the America of 1950, single-family dwellings were built with an average of 290 square feet of living space per resident; in 2003, a family moving into a typical new house had almost 900 square feet per person in which to ramble around.

Not surprisingly, monster houses are especially popular in Texas; in Austin, regarded as the state's progressive haven, 235 new houses of at least 5,000 square feet each were built in a single recent year; 41 of them had between 8,000 and 29,000 square feet. In the size of our dwellings, North Americans are world champions. The United Nations says houses and apartments in Pakistan or Nicaragua typically provide one-third of a room per person; it's half a room per person in Syria and Azerbaijan, about one room in Eastern Europe, an average of a room and a half in Western Europe, and two whole rooms per person in the United States and Canada (not counting spaces like bathrooms, hallways, porches, etc.)

The U.N. defines a room as "an area large enough to hold a bed for an adult"—at least 6 feet by 7 feet. That's not an uncommon size in many countries, but it's not exactly the kind of room that an American real-estate agent would be eager to walk through with a prospective homebuyer. . . .

To go along with those big primary homes, Americans now own 5.7 million non-rental vacation houses with a median size of 1,300 square feet; together, those second homes represent enough surplus living space to accommodate the nation's homeless population ten times over. Challenges to the oversized-house trend are being mounted across the country, most often on aesthetic grounds. Monumental bad taste can be morbidly fascinating . . . , but a far more serious issue is the lasting environmental damage these incredible hulks can do. Since 1940, the average number of people living in an American home has dropped from 3.7 to 2.6, but the average size of new houses has doubled. That extra space has gone partly to free children from having to share a bedroom, partly to accommodate Americans' ever-growing bulk of material possessions, and partly to make room for more lavish entertaining.

But if there seems to be no limit to the size of the material- and energy-hogging houses built in recent years, it's thanks most of all to that good old law of supply-and-demand run amok.

Wood Is Not Green

The current slump notwithstanding, homebuilding continues to account for a big slice of the nation's resource consumption. For example, the manufacture and transportation of concrete to build a typical 2,500-square-foot house generates the equivalent of 36 metric tons of carbon dioxide.

Construction and remodeling of residences accounts for three-fourths of all the lumber consumed each year in the US. In this business, there's no substitute for good old-fashioned wood. Laid end-to-end, the pieces of lumber required to build a typical 3,000-square-foot house would stretch for more than four miles.

In its review of the year 2004, the Western Wood Products Association (WWPA) crowed that "an all-time high of 27.6 billion board feet of lumber was used in residential construction, framing some 2.07 million housing starts recorded for the year. Lumber used in repair and remodeling surpassed 20 billion board feet for the first time in history." Consumption broke records again in 2005 for the fourth straight year, only to fall with the housing slump that began in 2006. Wood, unlike concrete, gets some credit for being a "renewable" resource. Spokespeople for the lumber and construction industries emphasize that they are taking greenhouse carbon out of the atmosphere and locking it away in wood-frame houses.

That's correct, as far as it goes; about half of the mass in a stick of lumber is carbon. But putting that wood into a house is a one-time capture, whereas the house itself will spend decades cranking out carbon dioxide and other greenhouse gases. Over a 50-year lifetime, greenhouse emissions caused by the standard American house account for 30 to 40 times the weight of the carbon that's socked away in its wood frame. The bigger the house, the bigger the emissions.

Furthermore, with the currently popular focus on the sheer quantity of greenhouse gas emissions, the ecological impact of uprooting complex forest ecosystems in favor of industrialized wood plantations doesn't figure very prominently. And a "green"-built house can require almost 50 percent more wood than a standard house of the same size. Hard times in the housing market will provide forests and the atmosphere at least a little bit of much-needed rest.

The current bust [in 2007] has already curbed lumber consumption, although WWPA expects demand to "rebound" in 2009. Meanwhile, the American Chemistry Council reports that production of the plastic polyvinyl chloride (PVC) fell sharply in 2006. Environmentalists have long sought to stem the highly toxic production of PVC, 80 percent of which is used in construction.

Size Matters

But, as environmentally significant as construction materials are, it's estimated that only about one-tenth of a house's total energy consumption occurs while it's being built; the other 90 percent happens while it's being lived in. That can be reduced by "green" construction, but making green houses too big can cancel out all of those gains. A 2005 article in the *Journal of Industrial Ecology* concluded

> A 1,500-square-foot house with mediocre energy-performance standards will use far less energy for heating and cooling than a 3,000-square-foot house of comparable geometry with much better energy detailing. Downsizing a conventionally framed house by 25 percent should save significantly more wood than substituting the most wood-efficient advanced framing techniques for that house. And it is easier to reduce the embodied energy of a house by making the house smaller than by searching for low embodied-energy materials.

Note the important word "geometry." To make outsized suburban manors more interesting, builders tend to avoid boxy forms, loading up their product with multiple rooflines and gables, dormers, bay windows, and other protuberances. Such houses have more surface area than does a squared-off house of the same size, thus requiring more fossil-fuel to cool and heat them. Additional energy is wasted by the longer heating/cooling ducts and hot-water pipes in a big house. For a given house design . . . the bigger its square footage, the bigger its environmental footprint.

A Question of "Want"

Although American houses have been growing since World War II, the low mortgage rates and hot housing market of the past decade are widely credited with pushing square footage to record levels. It's partly simple math and partly not-so-simple psychology—and it's all about money.

At the interest rates prevailing in 2003, according to the *Wall Street Journal*'s Jonathan Clements, you could buy a 40-

Smaller Families, Bigger Houses			
Year	People per Household	Square Feet per Person	Total Average Floor Area
1950	3.37	297	2,200 ft^2
1970	3.14	478	1,500 ft^2
2000	2.62	840	1,000 ft^2

TAKEN FROM: Art Ludwig, "Can a 4000 ft^2 Home be Green?" *Oasis Design*, http://www.oasisdesign.net/faq/green4000ft2home.htm, 2007.

percent bigger house and owe $273 less per month on your mortgage than if you were buying the smaller house at 1983-level interest rates.

Of course, noted Clements, you could show some restraint, buy a smaller house at the 2003 interest rate, and save another $281 per month. But the real-estate industry isn't all that interested in helping you downsize and stow the savings in your bank account or 401(k) plan. The question that the industry urges homebuyers to ask themselves is not, "How much do I want to save on my monthly house payment and utility bills?" but rather, "How much house can I afford?"

The heavy-breathing house market of the past few years added to the pressure by shifting many buyers' emphasis away from acquiring shelter and toward making an investment. Within a given neighborhood, houses are sold more or less by the square foot. So in boom times, the bigger and more expensive the house you buy, the bigger the profit you can make by selling it a few years later....

Demolition Is Not Green

Square-footage fever emerges in a doubly wasteful form in cities where normal-sized, sound, comfortable houses are being demolished to make way for bigger, more luxurious ones.

In North Carolina's thriving Raleigh-Durham-Chapel Hill triangle, demolition permits for single-family homes are currently being issued at the blistering rate of 42 per month. Speaking to the Raleigh *News and Observer* in June, the city's planning director described homeowners' motivation this way: "They have homes that are built in the '50s and '60s that are somewhat outdated for the lifestyle."

[In 2006], Les Christie of CNNMoney.com attempted to provide homeowners with an answer to the question, "Is your house a teardown candidate?" He advised that "even beautiful homes in excellent shape can be torn down," if they have come to be surrounded by larger ones. But taking a wrecking ball to your home-sweet-home makes the most sense when real-estate prices are running wild.

Christie used the example of "a little bungalow" in suburban Dallas valued at $500,000. The demolition cost would be comparatively trivial, and it would cost a builder about $600,000 to replace it with a "new, upscale house" of 3,000 square feet. In that situation, "if nearby new homes are valued at $1.2 million or more," economic logic dictates that the owner of a perfectly good house should tear it down and replace it—or sell it at a big profit to a mansion-building company that will demolish the house to get the lot. . . .

An SUV That Runs for Decades?

The long-term impact of titanic houses parallels that of gas-gulping SUVs and pickup trucks. Sales of the big vehicles may be ebbing, but the buying binge of the past decade means they'll still be out there by the millions, belching pollutants, for years to come. In the same way, even if the mania for big houses fades, Americans will be stuck with heating, cooling and powering the millions of them already littering the landscape—not for years like SUVs, but for decades. . . .

Very few houses now being built are as energy-efficient as they could be, and there is no good excuse for that. In one recent survey of 33 nonresidential green buildings across the country, their construction costs were found to average only about two percent more than what they would have cost had they been standard buildings. Built according to specifications of the Leadership in Energy and Environmental Design (LEED) system, the green buildings are predicted to provide energy and environmental savings averaging about 75 cents per square foot per year over 20 years.

Yet such prospective savings, if they can also apply to single-family homes, might simply serve the industry as yet another inducement that sells even more square footage—as in, "Hey, with this bigger LEED house, you'll get a couple more rooms, and it'll be like you're heating and cooling them for free!"

Clearly, the issue of mansionization will have to be yanked out of the tangle of other housing issues and dealt with as a serious problem in its own right. The individual question, "How much house can I afford?" will have to give way to the public policy question, "How much house can *we* afford?"

> "Land-use decisions made under the name of growth management will more likely hinder than help the development process."

Urban Sprawl Can Be Beneficial

Randall G. Holcombe

Randall G. Holcombe is a professor of economics at Florida State University and the author of Entrepreneurship and Economic Progress. *In the following viewpoint, he argues that so-called urban sprawl is not as bad for the environment or human beings as many critics claim. He describes the advantages and disadvantages of the three main types of metropolitan growth: leapfrog development, strip or ribbon development, and low-density, single-dimensional development. Holcombe concludes that these development methods will eventually solve the problems commonly associated with urban growth; therefore, there is no need for government intervention into how land is used.*

As you read, consider the following questions:

1. What, according to the author, are some benefits of strip or ribbon development?

Randall G. Holcombe, "In Defense of Urban Sprawl," *PERC Reports*. www.perc.org/perc.php?id=356. Reproduced by permission.

2. According to Holcombe, how can low-density developments help the environment?

3. What is the average commute time for individuals in the Los Angeles area, according to the author?

The term "urban sprawl" has a bad ring to it. The name reinforces the view that metropolitan growth is ugly, inefficient, and the cause of traffic congestion and environmental harm. Before we decide we are against urban sprawl, however, we should be clear about what it is and why we do not like it. Once we look at its specific characteristics, we can recognize their causes and what, if anything, to do about them.

My study of metropolitan growth indicates that three kinds of development are typical of what we call "urban sprawl." They include: leapfrog development, strip or ribbon development, and low-density, single-dimensional development. Let us look at each type in turn.

Leapfrog Development

Leapfrog development occurs when developers build new residences some distance from an existing urban area, bypassing vacant parcels located closer to the city. In other words, developers choose to build on less expensive land farther away from an urban area rather than on more costly land closer to the city.

Because land prices are lower, housing in these developments is more affordable. Some people decide to accept longer commutes in exchange for more comfortable, lower-priced housing.

What few people realize is that leapfrog development nurtures compact commercial development—retail stores, offices, and businesses. The empty parcels that have been "leap-frogged" create an ideal location for commercial activity. It is a fact of economic life that developers are reluctant to place new commercial buildings on the outskirts of an urban area because these areas lack a large market to draw shoppers from. When new development bypasses vacant land, however, the land in between is suddenly accessible to more people and thus attractive to commercial developers. Thus, leapfrogging is a vital part of development in growing areas.

Leapfrog development does create some extra costs. Infrastructure must be extended farther and the longer distance creates more traffic and longer commutes into the city. For a leapfrog development to be cost-effective, the outlying development must pay the full costs of the infrastructure it requires. It is the responsibility of local governments to see that the costs of water, sewer, roads, and so forth are charged to the development. As long as the new residents pay their share of the costs, leapfrog development benefits those who choose to live there and encourages commercial development at the edge of the urban area.

Strip or Ribbon Development

Strip or ribbon development, the second category, takes place when extensive commercial development occurs in a linear pattern along both sides of major arterial roadways. Like other aspects of urban sprawl, it is viewed as ugly and as a cause of traffic congestion, since shoppers and workers are often entering into and exiting from the street.

Yet strip development has its benefits. It brings together businesses that depend on high auto traffic. In fact, strips reduce overall traffic, since fewer cars must travel long distances from store to store or office to office. Strip development also creates natural locations for residential development. Between the commercial arteries, residential streets can have relatively little traffic yet be conveniently located near commerce.

In many situations, strip or ribbon development does cause problems, but the reason is poor planning. Every business fifty feet from another business does not have to have a driveway opening onto a major thoroughfare, creating congestion as

Interest in Smart-Growth Policies Has Waned

"Smart growth" policies, which became popular nationwide during the 1990s, are regulations designed to reduce suburban sprawl and control growth. . . . One goal is to reduce the use of the automobile; another is to create neighborhoods full of interesting "streetscapes"; and a third is to cluster people in high densities in order to preserve large areas of open space. Today, smart growth policies seem to be in retreat. Setbacks have occurred in Maryland, Virginia, and Oregon, and new census information suggests that the public does not really embrace the smart growth way of life. . . .

No one knows for sure what the urban/suburban landscape of the next few decades will be. But the latest evidence, including recent U.S. Census Bureau data documenting demographic trends since the 2000 census, suggests that the smart growth movement is having little influence on reshaping America's urban landscape. The demographic and economic forces driving metropolitan expansion seem too powerful to be reined in by the entreaties of smart growth advocates.

C. Kenneth Orski and Jane S. Shaw,
PERC Reports.

people enter and leave. Access lanes can be built to permit the smooth merging of traffic entering and leaving.

Nor does strip development have to be unsightly. If the right-of-way is wide enough, landscaped buffers can separate the road from the businesses. To achieve this separation, though, governments must plan ahead to secure sufficient rights-of-way for major streets before they are built.

Single-Dimensional Development

The third characteristic of "urban sprawl" is low-density, single-dimensional development. This is typified by large residential subdivisions. Houses are situated on relatively large lots, with only other houses nearby. Residents must drive nearly everywhere they go.

Critics say that low-density developments take up too much space, especially space that ought to be preserved in a pristine state. They say that they lengthen commuting distances, and, in general, that they harm the environment.

Low-density developments do take up space and may increase driving time. However, they have an important argument in their favor: People like them. Low density means more room and a higher standard of living. While every city has apartments available for those who prefer them, many people choose (and more people aspire to have) their own detached homes.

Low density is likely to help the environment. Yards filled with trees and shrubs absorb dust and chemicals, so smaller amounts of pollutants escape into the air and water. In contrast, in dense urban areas buildings, roads, and parking lots take up a higher percentage of the land, leaving little of the natural environment to absorb pollutants.

Government Intervention

As for single-dimensional development (that is, residences only), this is often the result of zoning laws. Some zoning laws flatly prohibit mixed uses of property. Prohibitions against leapfrogging mean that development on the perimeter of a city is mostly residential, since no business wants to put its commercial establishment on the edge of an urban area. Prohibitions against strip or ribbon development also keep commercial establishments distant from residential areas.

Thus, when the components of urban sprawl are examined, they can be seen as components of a healthy and efficient development process that is sometimes thwarted or distorted by regulations. I do not mean to imply that all instances of these development processes are efficient but that they can be.

Underlying all the complaints is what troubles people most about urban sprawl—transportation problems. Many of these problems arise because the government has not effectively controlled access to its roads. Traffic is clogged because there are too many access points to highways and because insufficient rights-of-way were planned to handle the traffic load. To avoid these problems, local governments should obtain adequate rights-of-way for roads, limit the number of allowable curb cuts, and require access lanes or separate access roads rather than direct access to thoroughfares.

Misunderstanding Commuting Patterns

Specific policies to stop or slow down urban sprawl reflect a more general vision of how metropolitan development takes place. Planners assume that suburban areas spread out from a central urban core. They assume that people work in the central cities, commuting from the suburbs. Growth management policies are designed to keep people living and working in central districts.

But this picture of metropolitan areas is not an accurate portrayal of today's actual commuting patterns. In Los Angeles, for example, only 3 percent of the total workforce works downtown. There are 19 major activity centers in the Los Angeles area, but even these areas account for only 17.5 percent of the area's total employment. Most people both live and work in the suburbs, and the average commute for individuals in the Los Angeles area is 20 minutes. While the statistics for each metropolitan area will differ, patterns in many cities are likely to be similar; today's jobs are primarily in the suburbs.

If left to its own devices, development will occur in a decentralized manner, which will usually lead different types of activities to be conveniently located in relation to one another. Decentralized growth will provide nodes of development. People can live close to the node where they work, allowing a more efficient pattern of two-way traffic as people travel between nodes. Decentralized development keeps commuting distances short but allows the amenities of suburban living for those who want them.

In sum, the invisible hand of the market guides property owners to develop their property in ways that result, over time, In efficient land-use patterns. When government land-use planning is examined, we find that land-use decisions made under the name of growth management will more likely hinder than help the development process.

| "The economic and social benefits of ur-
ban renewal far outweigh the national
drain accompanying sprawl."

Urban Sprawl Is
Not Beneficial

Carl Pope

*Carl Pope is executive director of the Sierra Club, an environ-
mental advocacy group, and the coauthor, with Paul Rauber, of*
Strategic Ignorance: Why the Bush Administration Is Reck-
lessly Destroying a Century of Environmental Progress. *In the
following viewpoint, Pope argues that local policies and an elimination of government subsidies to businesses that create sprawl
are necessary to combat the destructive nature of these new,
often-unplanned developments. He cites a number of solutions
that cities around the country have used to both allow the growth
of new communities and to preserve the environment.*

As you read, consider the following questions:

1. According to Pope, what are some of the environmental
   impacts of urban sprawl?

2. How much is sprawl costing tax payers in South Florida,
   according to the author?

Carl Pope, "Americans Are Saying No to Sprawl," *PERC Reports*. www.perc.org/
perc.php?id=356. Reproduced by permission.

3. What are three options mentioned by Pope for making smart decisions about urban growth?

On Election Day 1998, Americans from California to New Jersey voted to slow growth, save forests and farmlands, and rein in development. In an unmistakable signal of rising saliency and political power, growth and land-use measures appeared on more than 200 state and county ballots nationwide.

- In New Jersey, voters approved a 10-year plan to raise $1 billion to preserve 1 million acres of open space.

- In Ventura County, California, voters overwhelmingly supported an initiative to prevent local planners from rezoning farmland and open space without voter approval.

- In Florida, voters decided to extend the Florida bond authority to protect public land from sprawl.

What do millions of Americans know that Randall Holcombe's defense of sprawl ["In Defense of Urban Sprawl"] ignores? To begin with, Americans are reacting to the actual impact of sprawl on their lives, not to Holcombe's abstract economic argument that it could be good.

In fact, it turns out not to be good. Sprawl is a ubiquitous problem, and Americans—whether they live in urban Atlanta or rural Washtenaw County, Michigan—are deciding that current planning and development practices come with more costs than benefits. Development plans that may have worked fifty years ago are no longer the answer for today's growth.

Costs of Urban Sprawl

There are the obvious environmental costs of sprawl—lost open space and natural habitats, increased air pollution from more traffic, depleted water quality caused by urban runoff. Holcombe's argument that "low densities" help the environment shows an abysmal shallowness. He seems to assume that if yards were not filled with trees and grass, there would be less vegetation in the metropolitan area. In reality, of course, sprawl neighborhoods typically replace farmland or open space that was 100 percent vegetation and permeable soils and replace them with neighborhoods that are 30 percent or more concrete, asphalt, or structure with unvegetated, impermeable surfaces.

The worst environmental impact of sprawl is the least avoidable. Sprawl, by definition, fragments landscapes—and fragmented landscapes are the biggest threat to America's wildlife heritage. Sprawl is very good for the most adaptable and common creatures—raccoons, deer, sparrows, starlings, sea gulls—all do well—and devastating for wildlife that is more dependent upon privacy, seclusion, and protection from such predators as dogs and cats.

There are obvious quality-of-life problems caused by sprawl—more time caught in traffic caused by auto-dependent lives, abandoned urban communities, remote and isolated suburban neighborhoods.

But sprawl has an economic cost, too. Tax policies contribute to the public's growing dissatisfaction with sprawl. American taxpayers are actually subsidizing the extent and pace of sprawl through local, state, and federal spending, which increases to fund new development. That means a choice between more taxes or less spending in other deserving areas.

Sprawl Subsidies

Some advocates of sprawl argue, "Well, then just get rid of the subsidies." Holcombe blithely opines that "it is the responsibility of local governments to see that the costs of water, sewer, roads, and so forth are charged to development."

I wonder what planet he lives on. When localities try to charge developers even a fraction of the true costs, those developers and other sprawl advocates fight back fiercely. In

California efforts to charge new developments the full costs of new water supplies, which are far greater than those of the more efficient reservoirs built first, have run into tremendous resistance. In Alabama and New York developers are trying to hold on to federally subsidized flood insurance on the ground that it is a "right." The reality is that if we really got rid of the subsidies to sprawl, we would also get rid of sprawl.

The sums involved in the subsidies are huge. In Fairfax County, Virginia, a suburb of Washington, D.C., the 1997 budget of $1.8 billion ran a deficit of $146 million. In nearby Prince William County, taxpayers spend $3,838 to provide services to a single household, but only receive $2,150. A report released . . . by Rutgers University looked at the costs of sprawl to South Florida. Adding up the price tags on new land development, new roads, and new infrastructure, the report found that sprawl in South Florida alone is costing an astounding $6.15 billion.

Holcombe does not cite a single case in which the kind of low-density sprawl he defends occurred in the absence of massive public subsidies. He doesn't because he can't. There are no such examples.

It is not accidental that in the last era of metropolitan growth prior to the massive federal and state subsidies for highways, sewers, etc., the development pattern that emerged was of compact suburban developments with mixed use, light and heavy rail transit, and an almost total absence of leapfrog and strip development—America's streetcar suburbs from the 1900–1925 era.

Three Smart Growth Options

Taken together, these factors are fueling local action and a national debate. Americans are demanding common-sense solutions and smarter growth.

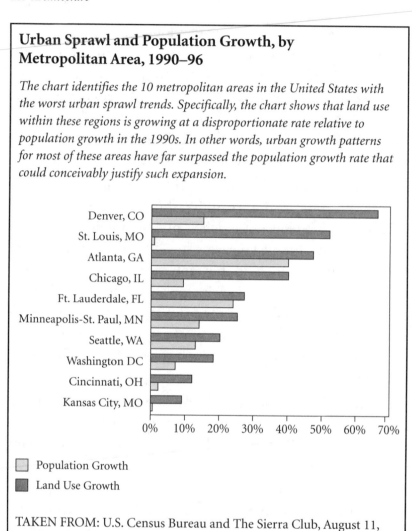

Urban Sprawl and Population Growth, by Metropolitan Area, 1990–96

The chart identifies the 10 metropolitan areas in the United States with the worst urban sprawl trends. Specifically, the chart shows that land use within these regions is growing at a disproportionate rate relative to population growth in the 1990s. In other words, urban growth patterns for most of these areas have far surpassed the population growth rate that could conceivably justify such expansion.

☐ Population Growth

■ Land Use Growth

TAKEN FROM: U.S. Census Bureau and The Sierra Club, August 11, 1999.

Fortunately, there are at least three options that provide guidance for urban growth planners charged with preparing plans for future growth:

- The first option is purchasing open space and farmland for preservation. Citizens in Peninsula Township in Northwest Michigan recently voted to pay farmers to keep farming rather than sell their land to developers for subdivision. Voters in Austin, Texas, supported an increase in water rates to raise money to protect thousands of acres of environmentally sensitive land around the city. Such purchase programs, ideally, could be financed from the windfall profits made by landowners who benefit from new publicly financed infrastructure. . . .

- The second option growth planners should utilize is marking and promoting urban growth boundaries (UGBs). Oregon and Washington states have blazed trails in this area by requiring all communities to design long-term UGBs. Portland, Oregon, has had an urban growth boundary in place since the 1970s. While Portland is one of the most popular cities in America and has witnessed significant population growth, its urban growth boundary has preserved open space around Portland and helped make Portland one of the world's most livable cities.

- The third option planners should pursue is reinvestment in urban areas and revitalization of existing towns and cities. In 1997 Maryland enhanced its existing planning requirements with Smart Growth legislation, which promotes state funding to priority growth areas such as existing municipalities and enterprise zones.

Taken together, these three options for controlling growth will help alleviate the costs and consequences of new development.

Left to Its Own Devices

Holcombe argues that "left to its own devices, development will occur in a decentralized manner, which will usually lead different types of activity to be conveniently located in relation to one another." This fascinating argument overlooks hundreds of years of urban history in which development, left to its own devices, prior to the era of either zoning or governmental subsidies, followed anything but a decentralized pattern.

Indeed, the classic original argument for both regulation and subsidy in urban landscapes was that, left to its own devices, development was too centralized and intense for human welfare. Freeways, zoning laws, and urban renewal were all developed to overcome the "natural" tendency of development to concentrate and cluster.

If there is any one constant in our history, it is our nation's ability to learn from our mistakes, to change with the times, to try something "new and improved." We have come to a new day in national growth policy. The economic and social benefits of urban renewal far outweigh the national drain accompanying sprawl. Americans everywhere are promoting a new approach to community planning, and the time has come for the planners to catch up with the public.

Periodical Bibliography

The following articles have been selected to supplement the diverse views presented in this chapter.

Maynard Barbara — "Going 'Green': Function and Form Key to New Home Construction with Environment and Energy Savings in Forefront," *Alaska Business Monthly*, May 1, 2007.

Economist — "Green as Houses," September 15, 2007.

Jerry Garrett — "Thinking Green, Not Pumping It," *New York Times*, March 11, 2007.

Robin Guenther and Anna Gilmore Hall — "Healthy Buildings: Impact on Nurses and Nursing Practice," *Online Journal of Issues in Nursing*, vol. 12, 2007.

Thomas Hayden — "'Green' Building Guidelines Go Residential," *USA Today*, October 1, 2007.

Marlise Kast — "'Green' Construction Becomes Second Nature to Building Industry: Environmental Consciousness Has Raised the Bar for Projects to Include Energy-Saving Features," *San Diego Business Journal*, April 30, 2007.

Kimberly Lankford — "Saving Energy from the Ground Up," *Kiplinger's Personal Finance*, October 2007.

Bob Miodonski — "Time for You to Take Green Building Seriously," *Contractor*, February 1, 2007.

Michelle Moore — "Green Buildings Matter," *American Prospect*, January/February 2007.

Tom Ramstack — "Building for a Green Future; Energy, Water Usage Being Cut by Design," *Washington Times*, March 18, 2007.

Beth Trigg — "Beyond Green Building: Expand Eco-Choice Outside the Walls of Your Home," *New Life Journal*, September 1, 2007.

OPPOSING
VIEWPOINTS®
SERIES

CHAPTER 3

How Can Eco-Architecture Be Encouraged?

Chapter Preface

Even though the growing interest in eco-architecture has helped lower the upfront costs associated with green home building by making environmentally friendly products and contractors more readily available, sustainable features still add 5 to 10 percent to the total price of new construction. While it might be easy to sell consumers on these added costs by outlining the long-term benefits, such as lower energy and water bills, some consumers are still reluctant to consider green homes. That might change due to the slumping housing market. With encouragement from realtors who are having trouble selling traditionally built homes, potential buyers are starting to think seriously about the advantages of houses that take the environment into consideration.

A May 2007 article in the *Wall Street Journal* revealed that the green housing market has not been impacted by the recent real estate slump. Consumer interest in green building products and green homes continues to rise even as conventional homes sit empty for months. To accommodate this interest, Web sites and other directories that advertise homes for sale are now updating their search engines to include green features. Even the mortgage industry is attempting to reap the benefits of this sector of the market by offering consumers so-called green mortgages. Major companies like Citi Group and Bank of America have special programs for homeowners who want to go green, including refunding a portion of the closing costs and offering rebates for purchasing energy-efficient appliances. Even some states, such as New York and Pennsylvania, are trying to help home buyers embrace green housing by subsidizing green mortgages.

Green homes have generally been marketed as being good for the environment and for human health, and now for the homeowner's bottom line. According to Eleanor Foerste, writing for the *Orlando (FL) Sentinel*, "Lower energy and water use and reduced landscape maintenance costs mean lower monthly expenses. Savings may even mean the ability to buy more house and still have lower out-of-pocket expenses each month." Elliot Johnson, an architect specializing in green construction, notes that homeowners can recoup the additional upfront costs for building green through energy savings in the first two to six years. Along with state and federal tax cuts for eco-friendly homes, consumers can easily recoup their initial investment and maybe even save more money over the life of the home.

Whether there is enough interest in green homes to keep the housing market afloat is debatable. As the authors in this chapter argue, encouraging green building is challenging and involves political, social, and financial issues. Perhaps the best way to encourage green growth is through word-of-mouth. A 2007 McGraw-Hill Construction survey revealed that 85 percent of green homeowners were completely satisfied with their houses. Perhaps this satisfaction, along with the total life-cycle savings and the promise of more tax breaks and mortgage opportunities, will be enough to maintain consumer and building industry interest.

> "Careful planning and keen attention to detail can reduce the overall cost for a new green building."

Building Green Is Becoming Easier

Patrick W. Rollens

In the following viewpoint, writer Patrick W. Rollens argues that the long-term savings of building green are worth the upfront costs. The basic costs of meeting Leadership in Energy and Environmental Design (LEED) guidelines are decreasing as awareness of eco-friendly architecture grows along with the demand for green building materials and practices. Rollens notes that not all sustainable building approaches will work for every project and that part of the resistance to eco-friendly construction is that most benefits are not obvious to consumers. Careful planning can make green building economical for most budgets, he maintains.

As you read, consider the following questions:

1. How much more does a building cost to meet basic LEED certification guidelines, according to Rollens?

Patrick W. Rollens, "The Cost of Going Green," *Fitzgerald Associates Architects*, August 1, 2006. Reproduced by permission.

2. According to a 2003 USGBC [U.S. Green Building Council] report to California's Sustainable Task Force, cited by the author, what percentage of life cycle savings will a 2 percent upfront investment yield for green buildings?

3. How many other green building programs exist in addition to LEED, as noted by Rollens?

It's something that sets architecture firms and development teams apart from their competition: sustainable solutions. The thoughtful application of various guidelines and principles results in green design, a forward-thinking movement that many architects and designers feel is the future of their profession. However, once numbers are crunched and bottom lines are taken into consideration, many developers balk at the dollar amount these environmentally friendly options can command.

However, a sea change is making headway in the industry. The accepted premium that architects and developers toss around is three to five percent—that is, attempting basic LEED certification raises the overall building's cost by three to five percent of its base cost. But even this amount is decreasing, driven by increased awareness and demand for green materials and techniques. . . .

First Cost Concerns

The separation of "first cost" and "life cycle cost" is helping to narrow the gap between the perceived costs of green design versus traditional techniques. Many companies are now working to help their clients envision the building's performance as many as 30 years into the future.

"Once [you] get on board with LEED, from that moment forward there's going to be a return and a value, and you have to get comfortable with the long term," says Randy Deutsch, a senior designer with Chicago-based FitzGerald Architects.

The US Green Building Council (USGBC), a nonprofit organization dedicated to promoting sustainable design, cites a 2003 report to California's Sustainable Building Task Force to advocate green building design; the report states that a 2 percent upfront investment results, on average, in a 20 percent life cycle savings.

That upfront premium is shrinking, too. The USGBC recently publicized five new LEED-rated buildings that all featured a zero net effective cost increase.

One such building, the 95,000 square foot Herman Miller MarketPlace in Zeeland, Michigan, was constructed for the bargain price of $89 per square foot. According to a publication from the USGBC, the gold-certified MarketPlace was constructed as a speculative venture that features individual thermal and lighting control, controls and minimizes water use and sports an HVAC [heating, ventilation, and air-conditioning] system that costs 40 percent less to operate than the industry standard.

"People are looking for ways to pursue sustainable design in a way that won't necessarily impact first costs," says Brett Mendenhall, an architect and project manager with Des Moines–based Herbert Lewis Kruse Blunck.

As such, spec developers will rarely pursue green design; the Herman Miller MarketPlace is relatively unusual. The impetus to try out sustainable solutions usually comes from owner-occupiers in build-to-suit arrangements.

Moreover, careful planning and keen attention to detail can reduce the overall cost for a new green building. LEED requirements such as proximity to public transportation or points for brownfield [a contaminated site] redevelopment can be achieved simply by picking the right location for a new building.

"At nearly no cost, one ought to at least be able to get over the minimum threshold for certification," Deutsch says.

Additional LEED points that can be pursued for silver, gold or platinum ratings can have marginal costs attached.

"When [clients] discover that they can get certification without adding a lot of cost, we've found that they are thrilled to go a little bit higher, even," Deutsch says.

The Right Decision?

There's no doubt that green design makes sense, but not all sustainable solutions are ideal in different building scenarios.

"Just because it looks like a sustainable idea doesn't mean it's a good fit for the project," says Thomas Taylor, a vice president at Vertegy.

His firm, a subsidiary of St. Louis–based Alberici Enterprises, works with companies and building owners to help them figure out the best way to apply sustainable building programs.

There are more than 75 green construction programs out there, says Taylor, and LEED is the one with the most publicity. When going for a LEED certification on a new building, for example, Taylor's firm works with contractors and developers to determine exactly which requirements they'll try to achieve. Some work for the project—but some definitely don't.

One example is a white heat-reflective roof. It's a great choice in Indianapolis, but it might not make sense in a building in northern Wisconsin that doesn't get as much direct sunlight.

Taylor's firm helps clients rationalize costs, but he wouldn't go so far as to say green design costs more.

"My response to that is 'more than what?' What are we basing this against?" he asks. "It takes a different mindset to do a green building. It's a different mentality that you have to assume if you want to be successful with it."

Green design decisions, he says, should be approached exactly as one might approach any other major financial decision.

"You typically say 'I have $100 to spend.' What's the best thing you can buy with that $100? You control the definition of best."

One aspect of green design that's hard to avoid is the commissioning fee. This cost, which accounts for as much as three to seven percent of the building's overall price, goes towards the actual LEED certification of the structure.

Obviously a building that's not trying to achieve a LEED certification level won't be saddled with this fee, but the practical outcome, says Deutsch, is that many smaller building owners who can't afford commissioning fees are unable to garner the attention that comes with LEED certification.

Visualize the Change

Green design doesn't usually offer benefits you can see and touch—and this is a major impediment to its application.

"If you tell a condo owner that they have an extra parking space or a larger living room or a larger hot tub, that's something they can immediately visualize," says Deutsch. The benefits of green design show up in elusive ways: lowered monthly bills, more energetic employees, a building that ages better.

The projected return on investments for a building's life cycle is a topic close to the costs debate. Some firms calculate their costs based on a 30-year life cycle; after that point, the building's amenities are considered paid for. Herbert Lewis Kruse Blunck, for example, tries to schedule a return in as little as 10 years, according to Mendenhall.

"It depends on the economics of the building," says Eugene Lisa, vice president of environmental training with Verde Interior Products, a Florida-based training and consulting firm. Lisa's firm works to educate interior designers, architects and developers about the attainability of green design.

Government Involvement

"There's something that's very interesting about this LEED movement: the federal government is behind it," he says.

The Costs of Going Green

As a cost consulting company, Davis Langdon analyzes the detailed costs for hundreds of projects each year. . . . One of the main focuses of Davis Langdon's research department has been to establish an internal knowledge database to serve as a clearinghouse of cost information for all projects estimated within the Davis Langdon offices. At the time of this report, the database contains information from nearly 600 distinct projects in 19 different states, encompassing a wide variety of building types, locations, sizes, and programs. . . .

As the various methods of analysis showed, there is no "one size fits all" answer to the question of the cost of green. A majority of the buildings we studied were able to achieve their goals for LEED certification without any additional funding. Others required additional funding, but only for specific sustainable features, such as the installation of a photovoltaic system. Additionally, our analysis suggested that the cost per square foot for buildings seeking LEED certification falls into the existing range of costs for buildings of similar program type.

From this analysis we can conclude that many projects can achieve sustainable design within their initial budget, or with very small supplemental funding.

Lisa Fay Matthiessen and Peter Morris,
"Costing Green," July 2004. http://davislangdon-usa.com.

The US government is the largest landowner in the world, and Lisa predicts that their willingness to embrace green design in federal buildings, military bases and auxiliary facilities will irrevocably drive sustainable design into the mainstream. "If the largest customer in the world is asking for greener materials, then the market is going to have to come up with those materials to be considered for business," Lisa says.

Moreover, he says, as the impetus is felt, the market will adapt with lowered prices. "As technology progresses and usage becomes more pronounced, materials become less costly," Lisa says.

The change is even percolating down to general contractors. Ingrida Martinkus, a LEED-accredited architect with Atlanta-based Thompson, Ventulett, Stainback and Associates Architects, says the initial learning curve was intense, but that's changing.

"Contactors and subcontractors are becoming more and more familiar with going for LEED certification," Martinkus says. "It's not such a rare item to be specifying green materials."

Martinkus' firm was one of the first architectural firms to respond to the growing demand among tenants for sustainable building designs in the US when they constructed a manufacturing plant and showroom for Atlanta-based Interface Flooring Systems Inc. The Atlanta showroom received a platinum rating for LEED-CI in 2004, becoming the first building to achieve the highest ranking for commercial interiors.

Ray Anderson, Interface's founder, became conscious of the need to put his company on a sustainable course after reading *The Ecology of Commerce* by Paul Hawken. Anderson has been spotlighted in the documentary *The Corporation*, and his company is striving [to] reduce its environmental impact to zero by 2020. *The Corporation* is a 2003 documentary that looks at the concept of the corporation throughout recent history up to its present-day dominance in people's lives.

Doing It Right

At the end of the day, clients and firms that start early and proceed through the design/build process with a sustainable mindset are able to budget their costs better than firms that attempt to "tack on" LEED requirements after initial conception.

"The only way to make LEED certification work and be economically viable and be done the right way is to start thinking about it from the beginning," says Jean Savitsky, a LEED-accredited senior vice president with Jones Lang LaSalle's New York City office.

She's currently working on One Bryant Park, a massive high-rise under construction in Manhattan totaling more than 2 million square feet. The development is seeking a platinum LEED-CI rating and a gold LEED Core and Shell rating, and she says costs haven't been prohibitive.

"If you do it the right way from the beginning, the costs sort of even themselves out," she says.

Savitsky's mantra has been the consideration of the building for the duration of its life cycle. She works with clients and tenants to ensure that sustainable design motivates everyone involved with the project.

"We're not just trying to slap a label on this building; this is a core value."

> *"Try to buy a green home in any major subdivision in America. . . . It's as rare as a flower in the desert."*

Building Green Remains Difficult

Auden Schendler

Auden Schendler is director of environmental affairs at Aspen Skiing Company in Colorado. In the following viewpoint, he argues that building green houses and businesses is not as difficult as most people think. Nonetheless, using eco-friendly building practices and materials remains uncommon. Schendler cites the building industry's unwillingness to explore failures as well as successes and language complexity as two possible reasons for this lack of interest. In addition, he contends that qualified talent and the freedom to take risks are necessary for any green building project to succeed. He urges consumers and builders to embrace sustainable design to save the planet.

As you read, consider the following questions:

1. According to Robert A.M. Stern, as cited by the author, how do most architecture schools teach eco-architecture?

Auden Schendler, "Raise High the Green Beam, Carpenter: Why Is Green Building Still so Hard?," *Grist*, June 8, 2006. Reproduced by permission of the author.

2. What are some of the obvious reasons given by Schendler for the slow growth of eco-architecture?

3. What is biomimicry, as defined by the author?

R ecently, *Colorado Company* magazine highlighted a developer who believes in nothing but "green" building. It was a wonderful article, but it gets at an underlying question: why is this still a story?

The idea of green building has not spread like wildfire. The mass-market building sector is oblivious. Most of the structures in trade magazines like *Architectural Digest* aren't green. [In May 2006], *The New York Times* ran an article in which Robert A.M. Stern, dean of Yale's architecture school, said, "I think the trouble with environmentalism is that at most architecture schools it's been confined to a dreary backwater of mechanical engineering." That is changing, the article reports, but not fast enough.

Coming Up Short

Meanwhile, even good green builders often come up short. In the environmental building community in Colorado, everyone's got a story of a disastrous effort: one that uses 10 times as much energy as it was supposed to; a micro-turbine that wasn't so cost-effective after gas prices spiked; a south-facing community college that needed its air conditioning retrofit in the winter.

Green building was supposed to be the road to the promised land, where good design meshed with stewardship for the benefit of all, while the bottom line remained intact. But if Moses were an architect, he would have come back from the mountain with 10 tablets of screw-ups and cover-ups.

So why is it so hard to build green? One response, of course, is that it isn't. In fact, there's a strong case to be made for a booming movement. Membership in the U.S. Green Building Council has grown to 6,000 since its founding in

1993. States and cities like Wisconsin, Seattle, and Portland, Ore., are adopting green building standards. There is reasonably strong federal action on the issue, if not at the level of the White House. And corporate leadership in the arena is expanding.

This all sounds good, until you look around. Try to buy a green home in any major subdivision in America, for instance—it's as rare as a flower in the desert: Some of the reasons for the slow pace of the movement's growth are obvious: cost; cultural and structural resistance; lack of talent or expertise; lack of research, funding, and awareness; and perceived trade-offs between quality or security and sustainability. But there are two less obvious reasons to consider.

Understanding Failure

The first is that stakeholders are afraid to challenge the myth that green building is cheap and easy. Once you've gone through the process, you're scared to point out the warts, because your work is now a model, getting enormous publicity. But ultimately, the lack of willingness to admit failure prevents the industry from learning from its mistakes. Until that changes—until there are conferences about mistakes and pitfalls, not brilliant successes—the learning curve will remain flat.

As renowned green architect William McDonough said after *Environmental Building News* reported on problems with the environmental studies center he designed for Oberlin College, these are new projects. The point isn't that they work perfectly at first, it's that they eventually work well. And, I would add, that we learn as we go.

Decoding the Language of Green

The second reason green building hasn't become more mainstream is that it's often discussed in a secret language, the code of a cabal [a secret group]. For instance, talk of "biomimicry"—the idea that buildings should be modeled on natural systems—is nearly inescapable. But as Michael Brown, an environmental consultant and editor at the *Journal of Industrial Ecology*, points out, biomimicry seems mainly to be about making something straightforward (avoid toxics, strive for closed loops, minimize energy) into something that requires a consultant.

LEED [Leadership in Energy and Environmental Design], the U.S. Green Building Council's certification system, has its own cabal-like nature too. The message is, you have to know LEED if you want to build green. But LEED is not how you get a green building—it's how you certify one. It is not a blueprint. If it's treated as one, then certification concerns begin to trump performance, and drive the process.

Here in Aspen, we're proposing new affordable housing that will run on lake-source heat pumps and use structural insulated panels. It would be very hard for this building *not* to beat energy code by 40 percent. We'll need things like passive solar orientation; envelope efficiency, including superinsulation and tightness; and an efficient and right-sized heating system. What we won't need is a consultant, a biologist, a Ph.D., or a translator.

The Need for Talent and Freedom

Successful green buildings depend on talent and freedom: qualified engineers, architects, builders, and owners, preferably with some green experience, who are willing to take risks and try new things. The Eastgate Building in Zimbabwe, which self-shades and dumps heat at night, isn't successful because it looks like a cactus (though that doesn't hurt)—it's successful because architect Mick Pearce is a genius, and someone gave him free rein, along with the help of a great engineering firm, Ove Arup.

But talent and freedom are in short supply. And that inevitably results in something that looks less like green build-

The Eastgate Building in Harare, Zimbabwe

The extraordinary Eastgate Building in Harare, Zimbabwe, is just one example of sustainable architecture that uses dramatically less energy by copying the successful strategies of indigenous natural systems. The building—the country's largest commercial and shopping complex—uses the same heating and cooling principles as a local termite mound. Termites in Zimbabwe build gigantic mounds inside of which they farm a fungus which is their primary food source. The fungus must be kept at exactly 87 degrees, while the temperatures outside range from 35 degrees (F) at night to 104 degrees (F) during the day. The termites achieve this remarkable feat by constantly opening and closing a series of heating a cooling vents throughout the mound over the course of the day.

Architect Mick Pearce used precisely the same strategy when designing the Eastgate Building, which has no air conditioning and virtually no heating. The building uses less than 10 percent of the energy of a conventional building its size. These efficiencies translated directly to the bottom line: The Eastgate's owners saved $3.5 million on a $36 million building because an air-conditioning plant didn't have to be imported. These savings were also realized by tenants: rents are 20 percent lower than in a new building next door.

Z+Partners, "Biomimetic and Sustainable Architecture: Learning from the Eastgate Building in Harare, Zimbabwe," Z + Partners (www.zpluspartners.com), January 24, 2004. Reproduced by permission.

ing than business as usual, with a green consultant thrown in. On typical projects, the consultant—to whom well-intentioned owners ascribe God-like qualities—is charged with jury-rigging an already doomed process. By, for example, helping to document that a building's steel studs and rebar, which would have been used even in a "brown" project, are partly recycled, and contribute to making the building bona fide green. (This is something I've been guilty of when using LEED.) These kinds of decisions, in turn, lead to mediocre final results that are hailed as "successful blueprints" for the future, and whose mistakes are never analyzed.

Change takes time, of course. But we don't have time. Buildings are a major contributor to atmospheric carbon dioxide levels, and we have to cut those soon just to stabilize them at twice preindustrial levels. As NASA [National Aeronautics and Space Administration] scientist James Hansen has said, unless we move aggressively to reduce emissions in the next decade, future generations will face life on a planet unrecognizable to us.

So it's well past time to think about how to speed up the adoption of green practices, and how to break down the barriers to a widespread green construction industry. We can't afford anything less.

| "Green architects are now paying no-
ticeably more attention to style."

Eco-Architecture Is Becoming More Attractive

Alanna Stang and Christopher Hawthorne

In the following viewpoint, Stang and Hawthorne argue that architecture can be aesthetically appealing and eco-friendly if architects and consumers are open to possibilities. They describe three sustainable residential structures in California that prove that green can be beautiful. Alanna Stang is the editor of Cookie, *a monthly family magazine, and Christopher Hawthorne is the architecture critic for the* New York Times. *They coauthored* The Green House: New Directions in Sustainable Architecture *from which the following viewpoint is excerpted.*

As you read, consider the following questions:

1. What is eco-banality, according to Stang and Hawthorne?

2. What, according to the authors, is the most remarkable aspect of sustainable residential design?

3. According to Stang and Hawthorne, what is Syndecrete?

Alanna Stang and Christopher Hawthorne, "Green, With a High Gloss," *LATimes.com*, June 30, 2005. Reproduced by permission of the authors.

What sort of image comes to mind when you hear the phrase "green architecture"?

If you're like most people, it's a forgettable one. For nearly all of its history, green architecture has been associated in the public imagination with earnest, uninspired designs that put ecological concerns ahead of aesthetic ones. The result is an architectural affliction critics dubbed "eco-banality": houses with misshapen sod roofs or office buildings with solar panels hidden away behind blandly conventional facades.

Two Schools of Thought

The gulf between high-design architects and ecologically minded ones has been, more than anything, a matter of divergent priorities. For their part, the leaders of the green-design movement in the 1980s and most of the 1990s paid little if any attention to the high-design or academic sections of the architecture world. Instead, they were determined to pay most of their attention—and perhaps quite rightly, given who makes the decisions about how and where to build in this country—to persuading lawmakers and corporate America that green design was a mainstream pursuit rather than an eccentric or radical one.

The architects most often celebrated in the design media and popular press, meanwhile, especially academics and self-styled members of the avant-garde, wasted few opportunities to denigrate green design. For them, as writer Susannah Hagan put it, green architecture had "no edge, no buzz, no style"; it was not only "populated by the self-righteous and the badly dressed" but "a haven for the untalented, where ethics replace aesthetics and get away with it."

Peter Eisenman, long a member of the architectural vanguard, had this to say on the subject as late as 2001: "To talk to me about sustainability is like talking to me about giving birth. Am I against giving birth? No. But would I like to spend my time doing it? Not really. I'd rather go to a baseball game."

Happily, though, the distance between the two camps has nearly disappeared over the last few years. Green architects are now paying noticeably more attention to style, understanding that without it they'll struggle to build a broad reputation in a design world that is increasingly preoccupied with image. Cutting-edge architects are coming around just as quickly, realizing just how much environmental damage the building trades are responsible for—and, more practically, that clients and building codes are demanding energy efficiency in new construction. The list of architects whose firms are now pursuing sustainability in good faith includes Renzo Piano, Norman Foster, Glenn Murcutt and the Swiss duo Herzog & De Meuron, each of whom has won the Pritzker Prize, the field's highest honor.

Perhaps most important, a new generation of young architects has emerged with little patience for the old enmities between environmentalists and designers; for them, the idea of a contradiction between architectural achievement and ecological progress makes little sense. As a result of these shifts, sustainability is being embraced by the same architects who set the field's stylistic and theoretical agendas.

Sustainable Residential Design

The new traffic between the realm of green and cutting-edge architecture is particularly notable, and particularly busy these days, in residential design. Since houses are small and self-contained, and often funded by progressive private clients instead of bottom-line-oriented commercial ones, they offer an ideal testing ground for new green strategies.

The most remarkable aspect of sustainable residential design these days is its diversity: of size, type, style and location. Green houses now rise from tightly packed city streets as well as hillsides and rocky seashores. They are single-family dwellings and subsidized apartments, primary residences and weekend getaways. They are sheathed in glass, in bamboo, in synthetic panels made from recycled newspaper. They take their aesthetic cues from primitive dwellings, from organic forms and, significantly, from architectural predecessors who include the founders of [1920s German design movement] the Bauhaus as surely as Thomas Jefferson, [Italian-American architect] Paolo Soleri or [American visionary architect] Frank Lloyd Wright.

Indeed, it's becoming impossible to ignore how many green houses are being designed in the sleek, ornament-free style that has once again become the prevailing approach among high-end architects, particularly younger ones in America and Europe.

Not surprisingly, Southern California, long home to the architectural cutting edge, especially in residential design, is helping to redefine sustainable design to new heights. Three recent projects in particular suggest the new aesthetic variety, and the new ambition, of green residential architecture.

Colorado Court

The largest and most prominent of the three stands near the beach in Santa Monica, its grid of 199 bright blue solar panels glinting in the sun. Colorado Court, a five-story, 44-unit apartment complex that welcomed its first tenants in early 2003, is the first large residential complex in the United States to combine advanced sustainability with low-income housing.

Designed by the Santa Monica firm Pugh + Scarpa, Colorado Court produces enough energy to satisfy 92% of its power needs. And it includes a list of sustainable features as long as any building in America, from age-old gestures like natural ventilation to recycled materials to keeping its tenants within walking or biking distance of their jobs and shopping.

The building's single-residency studio apartments, though small at 300 to 375 square feet, are a bargain by Santa Monica standards, renting for less than $400 a month. Pugh + Scarpa partner Angela Brooks suggests that low-income tenants are precisely the kind of residents whom green architecture ought to be serving—particularly in California, where the utility markets have been prone to huge price upswings in recent years.

"This group of people is the least able to pay for things like water and power," she says. "When utility bills go up, it hurts them much more than others."

From the beginning, it was important to the architects, who work squarely in the Modernist vein, that the building have some architectural panache. In plan, Colorado Court is made of three arms—two long ones on the outside and a shorter one in the center—that reach out to catch the prevailing ocean winds. In elevation, it has a precise, squared-off look, with outdoor hallways connecting the units on each floor. The deep-blue solar panels, made up of 5-inch square receptors, make the building immediately recognizable even from a distance of several hundred yards away. Inside, natural light, breezes and 10-foot ceilings help the units feel open to the outside and less cramped than their square footage might suggest.

Hertz's Working Laboratory

Venice architect David Hertz, best known for pioneering the use of a "green" concrete called Syndecrete, hasn't built residential projects at the scale of Colorado Court, but his work has been no less important in suggesting that handsome design and sustainability can be comfortably combined.

A perfect case in point is Hertz's recent addition to his own family's house in Venice, which enlarged it from 2,500 to about 4,400 square feet. Inspired by Indonesian architecture, it is executed in a style that might be called Balinese Modern, with mahogany wood stairs, trellises and other elements complementing exterior walls of concrete.

As a staunch proponent of green design, Hertz thought the mere fact of adding that much space, however much his

Green and Beautiful

When it comes to healthful home furnishings and beautiful interior color, Deborah Coburn of San Rafael [California] looks to nature. This design consultant . . . observes and follows nature's strategies. "Nature also has a way to make things disappear like the camouflage of a chameleon," she says. "So if someone has pipes, I can paint them out and they seem to disappear. When I do exteriors, I look to the palette of the site so that the house will sit quietly. . . ."

Coburn also considers re-use in her environmentally conscious design. "We already have enough," she says. "I like to design with what my clients already have so that the things they own become the things they love."

PJ Bremier,
Marin Independent Journal, *April 1, 2006.*

wife and children seemed to need it, troubling. "There's no getting around the fact that on a purely ecological level 4,400 square feet is a lot of house by most of the world's standards," he says.

His solution was to try to make the house the greenest house of its size he'd ever seen. "I employ green techniques in all my work," he says, "but I've thought of my own house—both the original and now this addition—as a kind of case study, even a working laboratory, for me to live with environmental systems, materials and methodologies."

An array of 20 solar panels on the roof help generate about 70% of the home's electricity needs, and other sections of the roof are given over to flat-plate collectors that provide hot water to the water heater, which then sends it into a radiant heating system in the concrete floors. Additional hot water

is provided by vacuum tubing on the roof, which uses a para-
bolic collector to focus the sun's rays.

All the wood used in the house has been sustainably harvested, and much of the concrete is Hertz's own Syndecrete,
which contains about 41% recycled content and is twice as
light, with twice the compressive strength, of normal concrete.

The material acts as a kind of "solar sink" inside the house
for passive solar energy transfer, storing up the sun's warmth
during the day, and thus keeping it from overheating the interior, and then slowly releasing that heat during the night.

Hertz hopes that by using Syndecrete in architecturally so-
phisticated projects he can help speed the adoption of recycled and environmentally friendly products to what he calls
"a high-end, design-oriented market segment" that in the past
has turned up its nose at green architecture.

Hertz's house, a stone's throw from the beach, features
some built-in natural amenities, such as cooling breezes that
blow in from the ocean and reduce the need for air conditioning.

The Brewery Lofts

For a green house in a gritty corner of northeast downtown
Los Angeles, Jennifer Siegal essentially had to import nature.
Siegal, who runs a Venice-based firm called Office of Mobile
Design, was hired by developer Richard Carlson to design a
house across the street from one of his projects, the Brewery
Lofts. It was Siegal's first full-scale residential project.

The lot Carlson had earmarked for his new house was
little more than a storage yard for scrap metal and other materials and bounded on one edge by the rear wall of a factory.
Carlson enclosed the other sides of the property with a 12-
foot-high wall made of rusting steel slabs. He told Siegal he
wanted to build the new house largely using the old metal

shipping containers, 40 feet long and 9 feet high, that he'd been storing on the site. It hardly seemed a recipe for architectural success.

Siegal began with a simple design gesture, stacking two containers on each side of the lot and then connecting them with a slanting roof and floor-to-ceiling expanses of glass. One stack of containers holds the master bedroom above and a library and media center below; the other contains Carlson's office up top and a laundry room and bath at ground level. Between the two pairs of containers is a living room with a flagstone waterfall and a kitchen to the rear.

Along with the containers, many of the other materials Siegal used were recycled or salvaged, including the huge Douglas fir beams in the living room ceiling, which came from a construction site nearby. Outside, the house is nearly enveloped by an extensive garden. Designed by James Stone, it features wandering paths, flowers and plants of all kinds, and an 85-foot-long stream.

The result is not only a surprisingly lush urban oasis but a spare, assured piece of architecture—and something of an essay on the hidden beauty of salvaged industrial materials. In that sense, the design by Siegal makes a fitting icon for a new approach to sustainable architecture, for projects that are environmentally resourceful and highly efficient but also aesthetically striking.

"*Rooted in outdated aesthetics and plain old snobbery, [anti-eco-friendly] regulations make less sense than ever on a planet in peril.*"

HOAs Often Ban Eco-Friendly Practices as Unaesthetic

Stan Cox

In the following viewpoint Stan Cox, a plant breeder and nature writer, argues that homeowners' associations (HOAs) restrict many eco-friendly practices, such as hanging clothes out on a line to dry, installing solar panels, and maintaining lawns without the use of harsh fertilizers, in an effort to preserve certain aesthetic qualities. Although some states have adopted laws that help protect the rights of homeowners in the face of various HOA restrictions, these statutes still exist because a majority of homeowners accept them and the real estate market takes advantage of them.

As you read, consider the following questions:

1. About how many Americans live in homes regulated by homeowner associations, according to Cox?

Stan Cox, "The Property Cops: Homeowner Associations Ban Eco-Friendly Practices," *AlterNet*, April 26, 2007. www.alternet.org/environment/51001. Reproduced by permission.

2. In the author's opinion, what is the purpose of National Hanging Out Day, observed every April 19?

3. How many states have laws that guarantee the right to erect solar equipment, according to Cox?

The house Heather and Joseph Sarachek were building in Scarsdale, [New York,] was to be a model of green efficiency, complete with geothermal heating and cooling. Even the electricity to run the system would be clean, coming from solar panels on their roof—but when the time came to install the panels, construction came to an abrupt halt.

A local Board of Architectural Review refused to issue the Saracheks a permit for the solar apparatus, having received a letter from at least 15 neighbors—among them doctors, lawyers and other presumably well-educated people—arguing that the panels "would clearly be an eyesore in our lovely Quaker Ridge neighborhood."...

Four months, $20,000 in extra construction and legal costs, and 107 petition signatures later, and after agreeing to plant a screen of trees to hide their "eyesore," the Saracheks finally got the board's decision reversed. On a 4-3 vote, the victory was a squeaker. But it meant that the prosperous Village of Scarsdale, where the average house is valued at $834,000, would see its first solar panels ever.

HOAs: Blocking the Green Path

On April 14, [2007,] in more than 1,400 locations from coast to coast, Americans rallied around the goal of reducing carbon emissions by 80 percent within the next four decades. On April 22, the *San Francisco Chronicle*'s Earth Day editorial spoke for millions of us when it urged, "The whole planet, with billions of people and scores of governments, must work together on the same page. It's the only way to curb the global threats of rising temperatures, dirty air and polluted and life-depleted oceans. One day in late April isn't enough."

But too many cities, counties, towns and subdivisions are still working off the wrong "page" by banning ecologically sound practices and even mandating consumption and waste. Rooted in outdated aesthetics and plain old snobbery, those regulations make less sense than ever on a planet in peril.

The Saracheks and other Scarsdale residents live under citywide architectural restrictions, but 57 million Americans—approaching one person out of five—live in homes regulated by homeowner associations (HOAs). These private groups hold sway not only in gated havens of the rich but in many more modest neighborhoods as well.

HOA boards of directors are usually elected by residents, but their architectural review committees often are not. They have sweeping powers to enforce so-called restrictive covenants, which can control almost any aspect of the property, from the size of the house or garage down to details like changes in paint color or placement of basketball hoops. When a house is sold, the covenant goes with it.

The Community Associations Institute cites polls showing that 78 percent of homeowners belonging to HOAs believe the rules they live under "protect and enhance" property values. And when it comes to enforcing neighborhood behavior, it's what people believe that counts.

HOA Policies

Many homeowners' associations post their covenants on their websites for the convenience of members. Doing some simple searches, I recently found and read a few dozen such documents. They are often highly detailed in describing what is allowed, what is not and what happens if you don't do what you're supposed to do or fail to do what they require.

I was looking for rules that affect a home's environmental footprint, and there were plenty. The most common restrictions were ones that prohibit drying clothes outdoors (effectively forcing the use of electric or gas dryers), forbid or restrict the placement of solar devices, dictate industrial-style lawn and landscape care or set a minimum square footage of floor space. Most also ban political signs, which itself can be an important environmental issue.

HOA documents are littered with those and a host of other bans on earth-friendly practices. Here are excerpts, taken directly from HOA covenants, that illustrate the kinds of prohibitions being enforced across the country:

- Westerley subdivision in Sterling, [Virginia,]: "Solar panels and solar collectors are prohibited."

- Camelot in Cottleville, [Missouri,]: "Exterior solar collection systems, wind generator systems or other similar appliances are prohibited."

- Peach Creek in Lisle, [Illinois,]: "Compost piles may *not* be created on any properties. . . . A window fan is never allowed to be placed in the front windows of a home."

- Quail Cove in Tucson, [Arizona,]: "Outdoor clotheslines are not permitted." (in a region where the great outdoors is like the inside of a clothes dryer!)

- Crest Mountain in Asheville, [North Carolina,]: "The following are precluded: Outside clotheslines or clothes drying . . . window air conditioning units . . . vegetable gardens . . ."

- Tavistock Farms in Leesburg, [Virginia,]: "Vegetable gardens must not exceed 64 square feet." (With no more than 8 feet by 8 feet for growing vegetables, should they really be calling this place "farms"?)

Sun Valley in Waldorf, [Maryland,]: "No awnings in the front of the house will be allowed."

Clothesline Restrictions

Suppression of clotheslines has probably received more attention over the past few years than any other type of anti-green restriction. Despite renewed interest in "solar drying," high-lighted each April 19 by National Hanging Out Day, HOAs across the country are retaining their laundry-line prohibitions—reflecting, say critics, their deep-seated prudishness and class bias.

People rarely confront HOAs directly over clothesline rules; most either conform or covertly disobey. Alice (not her real name) lives in the Lakeside Estates subdivision of Austin, Texas. Because her HOA bans outdoor clothes drying, Alice told me by email, she slips out to her back yard on summer mornings with one of those expanding "umbrella"-style clotheslines, puts it up, and hangs her laundry: "I put things out and try to get them in as soon as I can. I don't leave my clothesline out when it isn't in use."

Alice has received no warnings from her HOA—yet. But you wouldn't expect such guerilla-style energy conservation to be necessary in laid-back Austin. Alice says, "Yeah, usually people think of Austin and they think of relaxed attitudes. But I think since the housing market boomed, it has made people a lot less relaxed." . . .

Mandating Consumption

West of Austin, in more drought-prone parts of the American West, lawns remain the rule. Although xeriscaping—water-conserving landscape design—is becoming more common, one developer recently told the *Colorado Springs Gazette* that for the most part, "There's no question. People want green, nice, good-looking sod."

Even if they don't want it, their HOA might well force it on them. And environmentally questionable rules can intrude well beyond the front lawn. For example, by mandating minimum square footages, many associations are helping pump up the already-bloated American home.

A 2005 article in the *Journal of Industrial Ecology* showed that a very well-insulated 3,000-square-foot house consumes

Top Reasons for Using a Clothesline

- Electric dryers use five to ten percent of residential electricity in the United States!

- Save money (more than $100/year on electric bill for most households).

- Conserve energy and the environment.

- Clothes and sheets smell better.

- Clothes last longer. Where do you think lint comes from?

- It is physical activity which you can do in or outside.

- Clothes dryer fires account for about 15,600 structure fires, 15 deaths, and 400 injuries annually. The yearly national fire loss for clothes dryer fires in structures is estimated at $99 million.

Project Laundry List, 1999–2007.
www.laundrylist.org.

more energy than a poorly insulated 1,500-square-footer. And building a 25 percent smaller house saves more trees than are saved by using advanced wood-efficient construction techniques.

The average U.S. house in the 1970s had 1,500 square feet; by 2006, the typical house was heating and air conditioning almost 2,500 square feet, despite having fewer people living in it. The average home today has three times as much living space per person as in the 1950s. Many HOAs want to keep those numbers going up.

HOA Covenants

Here are some more typical passages from covenants imposed by HOAs in several states, each mandating some kind of stepped-up resource consumption or pollution:

- Piedmont community in Pine Mountain, [Georgia,]: "Size and square footage of heated and conditioned space: A minimum 2,750 square feet."

- Cobblestone in Wichita, [Kansas,]: "Minimum living area excluding the basement: Single level—1,800 square feet. Two level—2,000 square feet [with] central heating and air conditioning . . . seeded or sodded grass lawn on entire lot." Also "minimum of two car garage—concrete driveway" (no cobblestone driveways in Cobblestone!)

- Van Zandt Farms in Haslet, Texas: "Sprinklers shall be installed in the front yard of each residence."

- Eagle Point Golf Community near Medford, [Oregon,]: "Lawns shall be watered, fertilized and sprayed for weeds and/or insects and diseases as needed to keep them healthy and green. They shall be mowed on a regular basis."

- Applewood Park in Tigard, [Oregon,]: ". . . a mowed lawn that is regularly fertilized and is free of weeds and debris, . . . including clover and dandelions." (This is followed by a helpful hint: "There is a product called 'Bayer' that works well for removing clover.")

- Covington Estates in Fishers, [Indiana,]: "Each lot shall maintain at least two continuous dusk-to-dawn lights . . ."

- Franklin Green in Franklin, [Tennessee,]: "Each residence shall include an attached garage for a minimum of two cars and a maximum of three cars."

- Bent Tree West in Dallas, Texas: "Any garages, servants' quarters, storage rooms, or carports erected or placed on any portion of said lot must be attached to the main structure . . . garages shall provide a space for a minimum of two conventional automobiles." (servants' quarters?)

Penalties for breaking such rules can range from small fines to foreclosure and loss of the home. Anti-HOA activists maintain lengthy lists of cases in which families have been foreclosed upon—like the Orlando, [Florida,] woman whose house was put up for sale because she hadn't paid $108 in association dues.

The Peach Creek Homeowners Association guidelines, which say they "exist for the benefit of our community to help maintain property values," are typical, stating that a homeowner who commits a fifth offense and owes $200 or more in fines is subject to "legal action and/or forcible entry and eviction."

In an apparent attempt to provide some reassurance, the document speaks in the voice of Big Brother: "If a homeowner is found in violation of a rule, regulation or guideline and fined, remember this action is taken because the majority of homeowners in Peach Creek consider it to be just and proper."

Some States Crack Down

State legislatures are starting to rein in HOAs that try to ban environmentally responsible practices. At least 12 states have adopted laws that guarantee the right to erect solar equipment, although most of them permit HOAs to enforce "reasonable" conditions.

Hawaii, for example, passed a law in 2005 that ensures a right to solar energy. The legislation grew out of experiences like that of Matthew Calloni of Ewa Beach, who fought a yearlong legal battle with his HOA to put a solar water heater on his townhouse. And a bill was introduced in the U.S. House of Representatives in March [2007] that, if passed, will protect homeowners nationwide from HOA solar bans.

Many HOA rules forbid panels anywhere but on the rear of the house, flat against the roof. If the rear part of your roof doesn't face south or is in the shade, that's tough. Now before the Arizona legislature is a bill, HB 2593, that would prevent HOAs from requiring solar panels to be positioned inefficiently or in expensive locations.

Florida is one of the more progressive states in curbing HOA abuses, with legislation guaranteeing citizens the right to have solar panels, use clotheslines, and plant non-grass front yards, overruling any neighborhood policies to the contrary. Joanne Oliver of Ponce Inlet, was a highly successful realtor in Miami for 15 years. I asked her to imagine that she were showing a house in one of the upscale communities where she had handled properties and that the house next door sported solar equipment on the roof, a line full of laundry in the rear, and a front yard covered with tall native plants. Would that affect the price of the neighboring house she's trying to sell?

"Solar panels," she told me, "would not be a negative these days. And a different kind of front yard, yes, I think people might tend to go for that. That could catch on. But clotheslines!"—here, she couldn't stop laughing—"I can't remember the last time I saw a clothesline in Miami. That just doesn't happen. Wait, I have seen one clothesline recently—behind my mother's house in Ohio!". . .

Local Control, Bad and Good

When real estate values are considered as crucial as they are in the America of 2007, it doesn't matter what real people in real neighborhoods prefer. Players who have a big stake in the game have little tolerance for anything that smacks of green frugality.

Anti-environmental HOA restrictions are part of a larger problem: the growing power of such "private governments" to control people's use of their own property. But if the tide of ecological destruction's going to be turned, then flag-waving, don't-tread-on-me appeals to property rights, while helpful in some cases, will turn out to be a big hindrance in others.

If a neighborhood wants to outlaw four-car garages or ban daily lawn sprinkling during a water shortage, only the most fanatical property-rights crusaders are likely to object. But what if a more farsighted HOA decides to ban all toxic lawn chemicals or silence the shriek of leaf blowers in the fall (or maybe declare its streets off-limits to Hummers!)?

I'd want to live under regulations like those, and you might also, but there are plenty of people who'd fight hard for their right to blow leaves and spray weeds, just as hard as you or I would fight for the right to put a "Let's Get Out of Iraq" sign in the front yard.

A struggle to defend private property is always sure to draw broad support from across the political spectrum; however, resistance by environmentally minded homeowners will have to be mounted collectively and on the merits of the issues themselves, not just as a fight for property rights.

> "The LEED rating system . . . has proven to be a primary driver of the green building movement."

The LEED Rating System Helps Create Greener Buildings

Taryn Holowka

Taryn Holowka is communications manager for the U.S. Green Building Council (USBGC), a nonprofit organization composed of building-industry leaders who promote environmentally friendly building practices. In the following viewpoint, Holowka argues that the Leadership in Energy and Environmental Design (LEED) rating system developed by the USBGC is an effective tool for encouraging the growth of eco-architecture because of its holistic method of evaluation. In addition to explaining future changes to the LEED system, she explains the steps to certification and ways of making LEED projects successful.

As you read, consider the following questions:

1. What percentage of time do humans spend indoors, according to Holowka?

Taryn Holowka, "USGBC: LEED—Immediate Savings and Measurable Results," *Environmental Design + Construction*, July 12, 2007. www.edcmag.com/CDA/Archives. Reproduced by permission.

2. LEED guidelines evaluate building performance in what five areas, as cited by the author?

3. As explained by Holowka, what are the three steps to LEED certification?

Humans spend more time indoors than anywhere else—in fact, 90 percent of our time is spent inside. Buildings are human habitat—so shouldn't the spaces where we live, work, play and learn enhance our quality of life and the health of our planet?

The Case for Green Building

Every year, buildings are responsible for 39 percent of U.S. CO_2 emissions and 70 percent of U.S. electricity consumption. They use 15 trillion gallons of water and consume 40 percent of the world's raw materials. The air in our homes, schools and offices can be significantly more polluted than the air outside, and has been linked to illnesses ranging from asthma to heart disease.

That's the bad news. The good news is that while buildings contribute to major challenges like climate change and energy dependence, they are also one of our best solutions. Green buildings use an average of 36 percent less energy than conventional buildings, with corresponding reductions in CO_2 emissions. The impact is dramatic: If half of all new construction in the U.S. were built to achieve similar efficiency, it would be the equivalent of taking more than one million cars off the road every year. Even better, green buildings make sense for both the environment and the bottom line. Studies show that, on average, buildings that have been certified as green by the Leadership in Energy and Environmental Design (LEED) Green Building Rating System, cost a mere 1 to 2 percent more than conventional construction—and the investment is paid back in full within the first year based on energy savings alone.

But energy savings aren't the only story. Water conservation, reductions in construction waste, and effective stormwater management generate significant operational savings for the building owner, while also reducing the demand on municipal infrastructures.

The benefits to people are equally impressive—green buildings dramatically increase health and productivity. Anecdotal studies demonstrate that people in green buildings have 40–60 percent fewer incidents of colds, flu, and asthma; patients in green hospitals are discharged as much as two and a half days earlier; and kids in green schools increase their test scores by as much as 18 percent.

Transforming the Market

The U.S. Green Building Council (USGBC) was founded [in 1993] to transform the way buildings and communities are designed, built and operated. The council's vision is that all buildings will achieve sustainability within a generation. To realize this vision, USGBC developed the LEED rating system, which has proven to be a primary driver of the green building movement.

LEED is a voluntary building certification program that establishes a common standard of measurement for what constitutes a high-performance "green" building. Since its introduction in 2000, LEED has become a nationally accepted benchmark for leadership in green building design, construction and operations. LEED gives building owners and project teams a concrete, practical set of design and performance goals, and provides independent third-party certification that validates their achievements.

As of May 2007, 851 buildings have earned LEED certification, and 6,500 more are in progress—for a total of 1.1 billion square feet of building space. There are LEED projects in all 50 states and in 26 countries, and every business day another $100 million worth of construction starts registers with

LEED. Twelve federal agencies, 22 states and 75 local governments have made policy commitments to use or encourage LEED, and building owners and developers are increasingly choosing to certify their entire portfolios.

The LEED rating system addresses all building types and all phases in the building lifecycle, from design to construction to operations and renovations. Currently, USGBC offers individualized systems for New Construction (LEED-NC); Existing Buildings (LEED-EB); Commercial Interiors (LEED-CI); and Core & Shell (LEED-CS) [speculative development]. In addition, more than 6,000 individual homes and 200 builders are participating in the pilot test of LEED for Homes (LEED-H). LEED for Neighborhood Development (LEED-ND) has also opened for [a] pilot [program], and more than 350 projects have applied to take part.

LEED takes a holistic approach to sustainability, recognizing performance in five key areas: site, water, energy, materials and resources, and indoor environmental quality, with an additional category to recognize innovation. Four progressive levels of LEED certification—Certified, Silver, Gold and Platinum—are awarded based on the number of "credits" or points achieved in each category.

The Future of LEED

LEED rating systems are developed through an open, consensus-based process by USGBC committees. Each volunteer committee is composed of USGBC members representing a diverse group of practitioners and experts from a cross-section of the building and construction industry. Any USGBC member can serve on a committee, and all committee procedures and proceedings are available at www.usgbc.org.

USGBC is continuing to advance the market with the development of LEED Version 3.0, which will harmonize and align the versions of LEED, as well as incorporate recent advances in science and technology. Congruent with this effort,

Why Seek LEED Certification?

LEED-certified buildings:

- are leading the transformation of the built environment

- are built as designed and perform as expected

- have lower operating costs and increased asset value

- are healthy and comfortable for their occupants

- reduce waste sent to landfills

- conserve energy and water

- reduce harmful greenhouse gas emissions

- qualify for tax rebates, zoning allowances, and other incentives in hundreds of cities

- demonstrate an owner's commitment to environmental stewardship and social responsibility

United States Green Building Council, 2007. 3www.usgbc.org.

USGBC is introducing a continuous improvement process into LEED, which will create a more flexible and adaptive program and allow USGBC to respond seamlessly to the market's evolving needs. Particular focus areas include technical and scientific innovations that will improve building performance; the applicability of LEED to the marketplace, in order to speed market transformation; and the customer experience, to ensure that LEED is an effective tool for the people and organizations using it.

Life Cycle Analysis

The inclusion of Life Cycle Analysis (LCA) is an important step in the technical development of LEED. USGBC's Life

Cycle Assessment working group has developed initial recommendations for incorporating LCA of building materials as part of the continuous improvement of LEED.

LCA holistically evaluates the environmental impact of a product throughout its lifecycle: from the extraction or harvesting of raw materials through processing, manufacture, installation, use and ultimate disposal or recycling. USGBC's long-term objective is to make LCA a credible component of integrated design, thereby ensuring that the environmental performance of the whole building takes into account the complete building lifecycle.

LEED provides a framework for integrated design and construction processes, which are the foundation for building better buildings. Projects like Seven World Trade Center, the Bank of America Tower in N.Y. City, The Clinton Library in Arkansas, and Adobe's East and West Tower Headquarters in California are among those that have realized the economic and environmental benefits of green building.

"We already had a high-performing building, but going through LEED we uncovered hundreds of thousands of dollars of additional savings," notes Ted Ludwick, Assistant Chief Engineer, Cushman & Wakefield at Adobe Systems, Inc. "LEED got us from green to Platinum and it helped us teach everyone on our team how to stay there."

How to Go Green

Three Steps to LEED Certification

1. Register your Project. Register your project online with USGBC at www.usgbc.org. Registration provides access to essential information, resources, and software tools such as LEED-Online. LEED-Online is an interactive project workspace that includes templates with specific guidance on how to achieve and document the project's LEED points. Projects enroll in LEED by registering their intent with USGBC and

paying a fee of $450. Project certification fees are approximately $0.03 per square foot, and average about $4,500.

2. Track Progress and Document Achievement. Each team defines a "project administrator" that will serve as the primary project liaison between USGBC and the project team. Via LEED-Online, the project administrator can facilitate collaboration with project team members, share information and resources, and track progress towards the goal. LEED-Online also makes it easy for project teams to prepare and submit the calculations and documentation required to satisfy LEED's pre-requisites and earn LEED points.

3. Get Certified. The LEED certification process is paperless—all documentation and payment can be submitted to USGBC via the Web using LEED-Online. Teams can submit the documentation in two phases: First at the design phase, in order to get feedback and ensure that the project is on track for its goals, and then at the project's conclusion. A team of expert certifiers will review your project's documentation and a final LEED rating will be awarded within 30–90 days of completed submittal. Fees for certification range from $0.025–$0.035 per square foot for USGBC members. The average certification fee is about $2000, depending on square footage. The minimum fee is $1,750 for USGBC members and the maximum fee is $17,500.

Keys to Success

Start Early and Use Integrated Design—From the beginning, ensure that the entire project team is engaged. By establishing the project's sustainability goals from the beginning and pairing LEED credit targets with those goals, the entire team will work to achieve them. The integrated design process means that the full project team is engaged from the start and serves as an essential foundation for success.

Get a LEED Reference Guide—It may sound obvious, but many design teams simply hire a green building consultant without familiarizing themselves with the LEED process. Save time and money by learning what LEED points are available, which ones the project can attain, and learn about practical examples on how to achieve them. The reference guide is an easy to follow, invaluable tool.

Hire a LEED Accredited Professional—LEED Accredited Professionals (APs) have passed a rigorous exam and have demonstrated expertise in LEED and the integrated design process. LEED APs can be practicing architects, engineers, interior designers, general contractors, facility professionals or other professionals. Having a LEED AP on the project team serves two purposes—it will make it easier to achieve certification as well as earn a LEED point towards certification. Go to www.usgbc.org to visit the LEED AP Directory to find one near you.

People deserve cleaner air, a healthier environment, and a higher quality of life—and the building industry can make it possible. Together, we can make an impact: Every business day, $100 million worth of construction becomes involved with the LEED rating system, 50 people attend a USGBC training course, 20 people become LEED APs, and four organizations join the USGBC as members. Soon, we won't be asking if we should build green; we'll be asking why anyone wouldn't.

> "Basic [LEED] certification is too low a hurdle to merit the green stamp of approval."

The LEED Rating System's Effectiveness Is Dubious

Ted Smalley Bowen

In the following viewpoint Ted Smalley Brown, a journalist who covers business, industry, and the environment, argues that the U.S. Green Building Council's (USGBC) Leadership in Energy and Environmental Design (LEED) initiative is not an effective tool for promoting or even accurately assessing green buildings. Despite the press these guidelines have received, very few structures have been LEED certified and the certification process is costly and time consuming. Although LEED is improving, Bowen asserts that its overall effect has been to divert attention from true environmental concerns to meeting building standards that might only be green on the surface.

As you read, consider the following questions:

1. What is the average range of fees for LEED registration, according to Bowen?

2. How many member organizations does the author state are part of the USGBC?

3. What is the LEED requirement for city-owned buildings in Seattle that are more than 5,000 square feet, according to Bowen?

"I didn't like the 'LEED is broken' part, but I did like the 'Let's fix it' part," said U.S. Green Building Council President and CEO Rick Fedrizzi, referring to a critique of his organization's building-certification program that has been much discussed in green-building circles.

Published [in early 2005] by somewhat sympathetic sustainable-business advocates Auden Schendler of the Aspen Skiing Company and Randy Udall of the Community Office for Resource Efficiency in Aspen, Colo[rado], the not-quite-broadside comes as the five-year-old LEED (Leadership in Energy and Environmental Design) program is becoming the default green-building standard in the U.S. and establishing beachheads internationally.

A small but high-profile list of building projects certified under LEED has attracted abundant media attention and generated significant buzz within the building community and beyond. LEED is also rapidly picking up endorsements from businesses, state and local governments, and federal agencies, and accrediting a fast-growing number of building-industry professionals—more than 20,000 at last count.

But, echoing a growing chorus in the green-building community, Schendler and Udall contend that LEED is in crisis. They fault the program's cost, complexity, bureaucratic requirements, and what they characterize as a frequent disconnect between its emphasis on point allocation and actual environmental benefit.

Very Few LEED Buildings

The core 69-point LEED rating system addresses energy and water use, indoor air quality, materials, siting, and innovation and design. Buildings can earn basic certification or a silver, gold, or platinum designation depending on how many of the possible credits they rack up.

LEED-certified buildings are still about as rare as major wind farms in the U.S. So far, [as of fall 2005,] fewer than 300 projects have been certified, and about 2,200 have been registered, according to USGBC officials. Registration involves a fairly simple project description and a summary of the LEED credits the developer expects to earn, but actual certification requires thorough documentation, review, and commissioning, a process that can take many months and, some green-building practitioners argue, considerably drive up costs. LEED-registered projects accounted for just under half a percent of buildings constructed in the U.S. in 2000, and a little over 3.5 percent in 2003, according to USGBC officials. Those low percentages show how far LEED is from revolutionizing the building industry, critics say.

Problems with LEED

Many developers point to the expense of certification, rather than of green building itself, as a disincentive. The USGBC's fees for registration range from $750 to $3,750, and certification runs from $1,500 to $7,500, depending on the size of the building. But the big costs come in the form of energy modeling, commissioning, and other requirements of certification; these can run into the tens of thousands of dollars, according to architects and developers.

"There is a significant added cost to certification," Schendler said. He and Udall, who've each worked on multiple LEED projects, write that this can set up a zero-sum budgeting game, in which developers may forgo certification in favor of additional eco-friendly features. "In some cases it's a question of photovoltaics or LEED," he said.

Some critics also argue that basic certification is too low a hurdle to merit the green stamp of approval. They say developers can rack up the minimum number of needed points without going much beyond the requirements of local building codes and the efficiency standards of the American Society of Heating, Refrigerating, and Air-Conditioning Engineers.

Others note that LEED doesn't guarantee energy efficiency, as certification can be gained without earning many or even any LEED points in the area. Some green-building advocates would like to see mandatory points for energy efficiency. A point system that weights a renewable-energy system about equal with a bike-storage room needs some refining, they argue.

Seth Kaplan, director of the Conservation Law Foundation's [CLF] Clean Energy & Climate Change Program, raises the concern that LEED doesn't adequately address the siting of a building, which has impact on energy use, traffic, and pollution. "A building with a large parking lot that is full—on a fundamental level, it's oxymoronic to call it a green building," he said. A conventional building located in an already developed urban area is arguably more sustainable than a high-performance building in a previously undeveloped area, he noted. The CLF's LEED-certified headquarters is located in the heart of Boston.

Some industry groups also dismiss the LEED system as burdensome and arbitrary. The National Association of Home Builders [NAHB], which [in 2005] rolled out its own green building guidelines, and the North American Coalition on Green Building, which represents manufacturing and trade associations, have worked to counter the influence of LEED, claiming that it lacks scientific rigor and smacks of undue regulation.

Still, interested parties from across the spectrum recognize that LEED is the dominant green-building standard, so it can't be ignored. "It got to the point where if a project wasn't LEED, no one knew it was green," Schendler said. "It went from a kid brother upstart to an 800-pound gorilla."

The Results of LEED

The program's results thus far have been sorely disappointing. [From 2000–2005], LEED has certified only 285 buildings. By contrast, over the same time period, the U.S. Department of Energy's Building America program helped builders design and erect more than 20,000 new homes, with a minimum 30 percent reduction in energy use for heating, cooling, and hot water at no net cost.

We're concerned that LEED has become expensive, slow, confusing, and unwieldy, a death march for applicants administered by a soviet-style bureaucracy that makes green building more difficult than it needs to be. The result:

- mediocre "green" buildings where certification, not environmental responsibility, is the primary goal;

- a few super-high-level eco-structures built by ultra-motivated (and wealthy) owners that stand like the Taj Mahal as beacons of impossibility;

- an explosion of LEED-accredited architects and engineers chasing lots of money but designing few buildings; and

- a discouraged cadre of professionals who want to build green, but can't afford to certify their buildings.

Auden Schendler and Randy Udall,
Grist, October 26, 2005.

A Work in Progress

"We understand that as the definitive market leader we are the ones who are going to take those shots," said Fedrizzi, who sounded a diplomatic tone in discussing the tensions around LEED.

The USGBC's defenders are quick to note that LEED is a work in progress. "We're in our adolescent stage," said David

Gottfried, founder of the USGBC, the World Green Building Council, and WorldBuild Technologies Inc., a San Francisco consulting firm. "It's a maturation process."

The 501(c)(3) nonprofit's big tent holds nearly 6,000 member organizations—a diverse and sometimes fractious array of interests working through a consensus-based decision-making process. A self-described change agent pushing a voluntary program, the USGBC has been accused of trying to placate everyone, leaving too much flexibility in the system and opening it to manipulation. "We've always tried to be consensus-based and open," said Gottfried. "But, if you take that to the ultimate limit, you can get to a point where you can't function."

Industry players, some of them less than obviously green, lobby within the USGBC to influence the direction of LEED. They also campaign outside the organization to advance rival schemes like the NAHB's green guidelines and the Green Globes green-building guide and self-assessment program, initially established in Canada and the U.K. Both programs are touted as cheaper and more flexible than LEED. Critics argue they don't hold builders to high enough standards.

In August [2005], the USGBC voted to allow industry trade associations to participate as full members, a decision that disappointed activists like Bill Walsh, national coordinator of the nonprofit Healthy Building Network, a USGBC member. He fears this could tilt the council's agenda toward business interests. "Since every member of every trade association can also be a member of the USGBC, and often is, this gives some interests in the council two bites at every apple," he said.

Fedrizzi argues that the USGBC should be able to withstand the extra industry presence. "People have said it will force the organization to be a lowest-common-denominator organization. [But] if a group came in and decided to strong-arm the agenda in one direction or other, I have no worries that the members would protect the organization," he said.

LEED Is Spreading Rapidly

Even as debate roils about LEED's effectiveness and user-friendliness, the system is spreading rapidly. Federal departments and agencies and state and local governments are adopting LEED as a guideline or requirement for their own projects, and tax breaks and other LEED incentives are cropping up around the U.S. In many ways, LEED's success is raising the stakes and intensifying arguments over the program's flaws.

"We use it as a measure of our accomplishment toward our sustainability goals," said Don Horn, director of the sustainable-design program at the General Services Agency, the federal government's largest property owner and leasing agent. The agency pegs LEED silver as a goal for its projects, and requires certification as a minimum. "We've chosen to use LEED rather than coming up with our own," he said.

Other federal agencies, more than a dozen state governments, and almost 50 municipalities cite similar "why reinvent the wheel" reasoning for their embrace of the standard. That embrace includes requiring LEED for public projects and encouraging private developers to certify their buildings.

Seattle's LEED Requirements

"There are flaws. It might not apply as well to residential [projects] and location may not be emphasized enough," said John Rahaim, planning director for Seattle, which requires LEED silver certification for new city-owned projects of more than 5,000 square feet. "But it's largely proven."

Seattle's LEED experience hasn't been an unqualified success. Two major projects, a new city hall and a court building, have undergone rough break-in periods, necessitating some costly fixes to HVAC [heating, ventilation and air-conditioning], green-roof, sun-shading, and other systems.

Some of the problems involved building features that earned LEED credits, although it's unclear whether the problems indicate flaws in the rating system. "The issue of how we might better vet performance for the city's buildings has cropped up," said Rahaim. He suggests that monitoring be built into the system, to track how buildings hold up after they're completed.

But Seattle hasn't dropped its commitment, and in fact is now looking at adding LEED to its building code. City leaders have proposed that new privately owned buildings above a certain height or square footage be required to earn LEED certification as part of zoning rules, according to Rahaim.

Such proposals make some USGBC officials nervous. The organization gets a substantial boost from government endorsements, but it designed LEED as a voluntary program and doesn't want to play the potentially awkward role of regulatory enforcer. "We're not in any way promoting required acceptance of LEED," said Fedrizzi. "If somebody said, 'No building public or private will be built in the city unless it's LEED rated,' I probably would feel that that was not the right strategy. When you talk about government as an owner, they should have the ability to choose better performance. That's a voluntary action. Applying that to private projects is a different story."

The USGBC would rather help nudge building codes in a more sustainable direction, according to Fedrizzi. Thus, the group's "greening the codes" initiative, an effort to infuse codes with LEED-like requirements. "The building-code system needs to be upgraded," he said. "If it's not formally LEED but very green, I think it'd be wonderful."

It's Getting Better

Looking to maintain its momentum despite the friction in its ranks, the USGBC is working to address member concerns and refine LEED, while broadening it to cover more types of building projects.

The council is drafting and soliciting comment on a mushrooming assortment of new LEED specifications that will expand the system into homebuilding, retail construction, and neighborhood planning, beyond its current purview of primarily commercial and institutional buildings.

It's also collaborating with veterans of the LEED process to streamline its system for reviewing projects submitted for certification—an effort that was well under way before Schendler and Udall voiced their criticisms. Having already reduced the paperwork load with the last several LEED updates and pushed some of the red tape to the web, the organization will present more revisions at November [2005]'s Greenbuild conference in Atlanta. To expedite the certification of registered projects—currently there's about a three-year lag—the US-GBC is looking at phased reviews, a revised auditing scheme, and volume certification for builders, such as retailers, with multiple sites, Fedrizzi said.

Still, he admits, things are likely to slow down before they speed up, given the current backlog and the time required to revamp the process.

Beyond certification, the USGBC is considering ways to ensure that LEED-certified buildings perform well six months, a year, and more after they're completed, though details like penalties for noncompliance have yet to be worked out.

The council will also be spending time over the coming months trying to resolve controversies over polyvinyl chloride (PVC) plastics and wood-certification systems. Some greenbuilding advocates argue that LEED should encourage the replacement of PVC with more environmentally benign materials. . . .

And there's disagreement over whether LEED should give credit for the use of wood certified under the industry-backed Sustainable Forestry Initiative in addition to stocks certified by the Forest Stewardship Council, which is considered to be more rigorous. . . .

Both issues will likely be viewed as bellwethers of the group's approach to reconciling public health, environmental, and business interests, further revealing the hue and saturation of the USGBC's green.

Whether the council's efforts to adapt to the market while maintaining and even boosting standards will bring about the transformation sought by critics like Schendler and Udall remains to be seen. The concern for many longtime practitioners of green building is that the skirmishing over acronyms and checklists will distract from the larger battle to make the built environment more sustainable.

Periodical Bibliography

The following articles have been selected to supplement the diverse views presented in this chapter.

Consulting-Specifying Engineer	"How Do You Sustain Sustainability? Try Building Data," December 2005.
Peter Easton	"Funding for Efficiency," *Mechanical Engineering*, May 2007.
ENR: Engineering News-Record	"L.A. Policy Expedites Green Jobs," March 19, 2007.
Russell Fortmeyer	"Green Markets and Policies," *Architectural Record*, August 2006.
Alex Frangos	"Is It Too Easy Being Green?" *Wall Street Journal*, October 10, 2005.
Mark R. Heizer	"Industry Needs Baseline Consensus," *Heating/Piping/Air Conditioning Engineering*, December 2006.
Raya Kuzyk	"Going Green Without LEED," *Library Journal*, September 15, 2006.
Ronald Mahlman, James Clancy, and John Stauder	"Code Requirements and Sustainable Design," *Heating/Piping/Air Conditioning Engineering*, February 2007.
Peter J. May and Chris Koski	"State Environmental Policies: Analyzing Green Building Mandates," *Review of Policy Research*, January 2007.
Christopher Palmeri	"The Green Stamp of Approval," *Business Week*, September 11, 2006.
Michael Stoll	"A Green Agenda for Cities," *E: The Environmental Magazine*, September/October 2005.
Amanda Webb	"Cities Begin Requiring Private Developers to Go Green—With and Without LEED," *Architectural Record*, February 2007.

OPPOSING
VIEWPOINTS®
SERIES

CHAPTER 4

How Is Eco-Architecture Being Implemented?

Chapter Preface

Despite the growing interest in eco-architecture, consumers and even building industry professionals remain confused about just what it means to be green. Given that a number of organizations, including the U.S. Green Building Council, Green Globes, and the National Association of Homebuilders, have established their own green guidelines, defining "true green" is challenging, even for most eco-experts. Regrettably, this lack of clarity has led to varying degrees of green building that in the end might not add up to much in terms of lessening the impact of these structures on the environment.

Although most green-building experts agree on some of the larger goals of eco-architecture, such as conserving scarce resources, reducing harmful effects on occupants, and saving energy, the specifics on how these goals are accomplished is the puzzling part. Most building companies rely on product manufacturers and outside agencies to certify materials as eco-friendly, and many of the guidelines for certification are not regulated by objective, third-party organizations. In the end, industry professionals often base their decisions on cost. In an article in *City Limits Magazine*, Elizabeth Cady Brown notes, "The green building movement has made the marketplace its battleground in part because of who leads it: mid-career, middle-aged building industry professionals. While they hail from varied fields—including construction, architecture, engineering, manufacturing, real estate and development—they are all accustomed to making decisions based on the bottom line."

Some critics have argued that the majority of companies who have entered the green housing market have done so with limited views on what it means for buildings to be truly environmentally friendly. Eco-activist Don Fitz has argued that most building industry experts are more interested in finding expensive, quick-fix solutions to energy issues than they are in thinking carefully about how best to use the site on which the building will be constructed. He argues, "The architects and builders I have met seem to be sincere people who are trying to do the best they can. But most jump to expensive green gadgets or efficiency systems before looking for low-tech solutions." Low-tech solutions can include attic fans instead of central air systems and clotheslines instead of clothes dryers.

Given that buildings contribute more than 40 percent of all of the carbon emissions in the United States alone, it is no wonder that so much attention is being paid to the impact they have on the environment. The challenge is in finding a way to ensure that green buildings really are green and not simply greenwashed to appease consumer interests. As the authors in this chapter argue, encouraging varied and creative approaches to eco-architecture is important to its continued growth, but a better system of regulation might be needed to ensure that green buildings really are green.

| "The sustainability movement is no
  longer a niche thing at most colleges."

More College Campuses Are Building Green

Timothy Egan

Timothy Egan is a Pulitzer Prize-winning author of five books that focus on the environment and politics of the western United States. In the following viewpoint, he argues that eco-friendly practices are no longer a fad on most college campuses. He asserts that college administrators have realized that going green not only saves the environment but also their bottom line. Citing examples from across the country, Egan explains that these green efforts are also popular among students and faculty, who have largely embraced the sustainability movement.

As you read, consider the following questions:

1. How many colleges around the country have built or are building structures certified by the USGBC, according to Egan?

Timothy Egan, "The Greening of America's Campuses," *The New York Times,* January 8, 2006. Copyright © 2006 by The New York Times Company. Reproduced by permission of the publisher and author.

2. As reported by the author, by what percentage did the University of South Carolina reduce its heating and electricity costs in its new eco-friendly residence hall compared with a traditional dormitory?

3. What characteristics make the roof of Carnegie Mellon University's Hamerschlag Hall a "living roof," according to Egan?

The largest university in Oregon is camouflaged, its many parts spread among the tight urban canyons of downtown Portland. But one building at Portland State University stands out. It has a roof of grass, plants and gravel, like a slice of the high desert on the wet side of Oregon. It is 10 stories high, and inside, all the mechanical organs work with so little waste—pumping water, air and electricity to the 400 residents of the dormitory and, on lower floors, to classrooms—that it would impress even the thrifty New Englanders who founded Portland.

If it is true, as Winston Churchill said, that "we shape our dwellings, and afterwards our dwellings shape us," then Portland State's new residence hall, the Broadway, may be more than environmentally virtuous. Open barely a year, it is attracting students who say they want their campus home to be a living laboratory, even if that means low-flow showers are part of a 24-hour classroom. "This building is really cool, and everybody likes being a part of it," says Micaiah Fifer, a junior who lives in the Broadway. "I appreciate the fact that this school is trying to be environmentally friendly. It's a reason to like the school."

The low water pressure, he admits, "gets to be a little annoying." Still, students are lining up to take on such challenges. More than a hundred students at the University of South Carolina, Columbia, were on the waiting list [in 2005] for what is being promoted as the world's largest green dorm.

Students had to write an essay stating why they wanted to live in the building, which opened in fall 2004.

Green Credentials

Colleges have long marketed their campus amenities, their rosters of scholars, their selectivity and study-abroad programs. To that list, add one more thing: their green credentials.

From Berea College in Kentucky, where students designed a house that produces its own electricity, to Middlebury in Vermont, where local forests supply wood for construction, the greening of higher education is everywhere, showing signs of outlasting earlier, faddish fits and starts. Nationwide, more than 110 colleges have built or are building structures certified by the United States Green Building Council, a nonprofit group that promotes construction and designs that meet high standards of energy efficiency.

But it's one thing to put up a trophy of recycled glass and brick that relies on the sun, the wind or other renewable resources for power. It's another to build a curriculum—and to get students to look at the world differently—with green buildings as a centerpiece.

In Pittsburgh, students at Carnegie Mellon study the weave of grass, dirt and bugs atop its new "living roof" at Hamerschlag Hall. In class projects they study how the building design can reduce storm water drainage and improve water quality. Yavapai College in Arizona and Harvey Mudd College in California have built classes around new ways to use the earth's resources, with campus designs as the prime exhibits.

Sustainability Catches On

The students, professors and designers behind this movement say they are part of a broad push for sustainability, which has become a buzzword for new schools of thought in architecture, interior design, urban planning, culinary arts and other fields. At its simplest, sustainability means taking as little as possible from resources that cannot be renewed. A movement without real leaders, it seems to have the greatest resonance on college campuses, always a home for new thinking. Student groups and sessions dedicated to sustainability are flourishing. While some produce little but conversational—and political— gas, others are preaching practical solutions. At Drury University in Missouri, a campus conference on using natural resources ended with a posting of "10 simple ways to support sustainable living in the Ozarks." Among the suggestions: shop at local food producers.

At [2005]'s annual conference of the Society for College and University Planning, green buildings and ideas on how to spread eco-friendly practices dominated many discussions. With studies showing that students perform better in buildings with better (natural) light and cleaner circulating air, universities are taking their campuses out of the dark ages.

"What university leaders are telling us is that they now see this as an opportunity for recruitment," says Rick Fedrizzi, president of the Green Building Council. "It signals to the potential student that this is an organization that gets it."

Because living lighter can save money, administrators say, they can—as the old line about prosperous missionaries has it—do well while trying to do good. With energy prices at record highs, and many economists predicting the end of the oil age within a generation's time, the college sustainability movement could play a big role outside the academic bubble. For example, by using lots of windows, mirrors and a big bank of photovoltaic cells, which convert sunlight to electricity, the University of South Carolina has reduced heating costs in its new residence hall by 20 percent and electricity costs by 40 percent, compared with a similarly sized dorm. The system is the largest on the East Coast, university officials say, and shows that even a large apartment building can use a clean, renewable source of energy at relatively low cost.

Going Beyond a Fad

"The sustainability movement is no longer a niche thing at most colleges," says Peggy F. Barlett, an anthropology professor at Emory University in Atlanta, who edited, with Geoffrey W. Chase, a book of essays on the subject. "There's going to be a real cultural transformation in the coming years in this area."

Ms. Barlett was behind the Piedmont Project, an effort to bring green sensibility to all parts of Emory. It started slowly, [in 2000], but has lately taken off because of high energy costs and the desire of students and teachers to turn their ideas into practicality. Atlanta's environmental problems—stagnant air and poor water quality, sprawl, horrendous traffic jams—also prompted many on campus to take another look at their relationship with the natural world, she says.

The Piedmont Project involves little things (a literary class on eco-criticism, a student project on maintaining golf courses using minimal amounts of water and chemicals) and big things (two new green-certified buildings that are under construction).

The project was inspired by the pioneering Northern Arizona University, in the high pine-forested reach of Flagstaff. With its proximity to some of the world's most stunning scenery, Flagstaff, which attracts lovers of outdoor sports, has consistently been rated among the nation's most livable medium-size cities. The university has tried to match the setting.

"Kids who spend a lot of their time in national parks and outside are going to want to live in a campus that reflects their values," says Gary Paul Nabhan, director of the university's Center for Sustainable Environments. "A huge portion of our student body is motivated to be engaged in environmental issues."

Conferences, classrooms and buildings try to reflect this ethic. Administrators have declared that every new building must meet some degree of green construction and design standards, meaning that they use a high percentage of recycled building materials and incorporate low-energy-using lighting and electrical systems. Solar panels are abundant, making use of the sun at Flagstaff's altitude of 7,000 feet.

Even the janitors and land maintenance crews have been brought aboard. "Rather than a bunch of academics and student activists trying to ram some ideas down people's throats," says Dr. Nabhan, who is also a professor of environmental science, "we let the people who work on campus come up with ideas about how to use less, and we listen to them."

Pittsburgh Goes Green

It was not so long ago when what fell from the sky in Pittsburgh caused people to rush indoors or cough. Soot and ash from the mills that gave the city its nickname, Steeltown, U.S.A., could block the sun and discolor clothes. But in the nearly two decades since the mills were shuttered, Pittsburgh has remade itself, with one of the city's best-known universities, Carnegie Mellon, in the forefront.

The living roof of Hamerschlag Hall sprouted four years ago from a "why not?" idea of three students who were members of the campus Sustainable Earth Club. With an undergraduate research grant, the students studied other green roofs and drew up a general plan; students of architecture and engineering in an advanced sculpture studio class designed it [in 2005].

The roof, which cost $172,000, is a showpiece, with its grasses, perennials and a log drilled with holes to encourage insects to settle in. Instruments were installed to measure water runoff, water quality, and heat loss and retention in the building, with monitors installed on a traditional roof nearby so data could be compared.

Elsewhere on campus, the energy-saving gadgets and systems of New House—the first green dormitory to open in the country, according to Carnegie Mellon officials—have also be-

Conservation on Campuses in Washington State

Colleges in Washington are trying to improve sustainability efforts throughout campus.

Food: Campus eateries are serving locally grown foods, organic fruits and vegetables and fair-trade coffee. . . .

Campus construction: Universities are voluntarily seeking certification from the U.S. Green Building Council, which requires buildings to meet certain sustainable construction standards. . . .

Energy consumption: Universities are paying more for renewable energy generated by dams and wind farms. . . . Colleges are also exploring other energy options, such as biodiesel and solar power.

Recycle and reuse: Many universities recycle paper, aluminum, glass and plastic. They're also encouraging students to donate unwanted items instead of throwing them in the trash bin. . . .

Classroom: Students at Washington State University can major in organic farming. The UW student government [in 2006] passed a "green textbook" resolution asking the university to lobby textbook publishers to produce materials with more recycled paper.

Christine Frey,
Seattle Post Intelligencer, *August 23, 2006.*

come teaching tools. Now [in 2006] in its third year, the five-story, 260-bed residence uses 30 percent less energy than a typical building of the same size, and it came in under budget. A kiosk shows the daily energy use and compares it with previous days, making students aware of their daily impact on the resources needed to house them. Carpets are made of recycled fiber and the doors were certified by sustainable forestry groups. Campus environmental groups use New House as a home.

"This is very much a living laboratory," says Tim Michael, director of housing and dining services at Carnegie Mellon. "The building is constantly being studied by students, architects and engineers." He says Carnegie Mellon is moving toward applying the same stringent green-building standards to all its major new construction.

Beyond the well-insulated walls of New House, Carnegie Mellon has been trying to integrate sustainable theory in many aspects of campus life and curriculum. Teachers at the new Center for Sustainable Engineering, in collaboration with like-minded colleagues at the University of Texas and Arizona State University, want to revolutionize teaching at the nation's 1,500 engineering programs. Supported by a $1.7 million grant from the National Science Foundation, the center holds workshops and develops educational materials meant to get students to think about energy efficiency and recycled material.

"The whole purpose of this is to take some of the ideas of sustainability out of the fringes and put them into the mainstream," says Cliff Davidson, a professor in civil and environmental engineering and a co-founder of the center.

University of South Carolina's West Quad

It helps to have a shiny new example of what all the fuss is about. That is the case with the University of South Carolina's new residence hall, West Quad, which has been certified by the environment-friendly building council. About 500 students live in the complex of three four-story buildings, which includes a learning center where classes on the environment are taught.

There is a perception that a green dorm is going to force a monastic life on students, but West Quad residents insist they are not uncomfortable. No cold showers or dimly lighted study halls, they say.

"The thing I notice most is the air quality," says Lindsey Cooper, a graduate student who lives at West Quad. "They are constantly filtering in new air. And the lighting is so reliant on natural lights that I don't even feel like I use electric lights very much."

West Quad has become the iPod of buildings. "It's clearly the most popular hall on campus," says Gene Luna, a university vice president. Plans are under way to build a green fraternity house.

As at Carnegie Mellon, the building is a learning opportunity. Biology majors have experimented with different plants, trying to create an attractive landscape that uses a minimal amount of water. Engineering students monitor the energy output provided by simple daylight to heat all those hot showers.

"This building has just exceeded our expectations in every way," Dr. Luna says. "You can't traverse across the West Quad complex without learning something."

> *"The environmental, academic, finan-*
> *cial, and health benefits [of green*
> *schools] are impossible to ignore."*

School Districts Are Learning the Benefits of Eco-Architecture

Debra Lau Whelan

Debra Lau Whelan is senior news and features editor at School Library Journal *in which the following viewpoint appeared. Whelan argues that more schools across the country are adopting green building practices because the benefits are obvious. Not only do eco-friendly building practices help save the environment but they also save school districts money in the long run in both energy savings and health benefits for employees. In addition, the U.S. Green Building Council adopted Leadership in Energy and Environmental Design guidelines that specifically focus on schools, which has encouraged even more districts to explore green options.*

As you read, consider the following questions:

1. How many schools across the country have gone completely green, according to Whelan?

Debra Lau Whelan, "Going Green: Eco-Friendly Schools," *School Library Journal*, September 1, 2007. Reproduced from *School Library Journal*. A Cahners/R. R. Bowker Publication, by permission.

2. According to the author, what fraction of the schools in the United States have indoor air quality problems?

3. About how much per year can building a green school save, according to Whelan?

Maybe it's the waterless urinals or the geothermal heating and cooling system buried 515 feet underground. Or perhaps it's the motion-activated faucets or the paints and furnishings made from low-volatile organic compounds. But one thing's for sure: Great Seneca Creek Elementary is unlike most schools.

Since opening its doors in the fall of 2006, this school in Germantown, [Maryland], has hosted more than two dozen tours for administrators, architects, parents, and the media—just about anyone who's interested in studying its environmentally-friendly ways. "It's a place where people feel they can do their work more effectively, because it's an environment they want to be in," says Principal Greg Edmundson about his school, the only one in the state to receive certification from the U.S. Green Building Council (USGBC).

The folks at Fossil Ridge High School in Fort Collins, [Colorado,] know exactly what he's talking about. Their 296,000-square-foot building—which runs on wind and solar power and boasts an irrigation pond—recently earned a silver rating from USGBC's Leadership in Energy and Environmental Design (LEED) Green Building Rating System, a rigorous set of national standards for environmentally sustainable construction. "This is a dream building," says Fossil Ridge's media specialist, Lana Fain. "My students have told me that the space and lighting makes it easier for them to focus. They just love being here."

Benefits Impossible to Ignore

Some 50 schools, from California to Maine, have gone totally green—and hundreds more will soon follow suit. Why is eco-friendly design one of the hottest trends in K-12 education?

Because the environmental, academic, financial, and health benefits are impossible to ignore, says Bob Moje, president of the Charlottesville, VA–based VMDO Architects, which mainly serves the school and university market. "People are more enlightened now about why it's good to be green," he says about the change in attitude of his clients over the last five years [2002–2007]. "We've gone from people saying, 'We don't want to be different' to 'We don't want to be left out.'"

It's easy to understand why. On average, green schools use 33 percent less energy and 32 percent less water, according to USGBC. Seneca Creek, for instance, skims about $60,000 off its annual energy bill and conserves about 43 percent—or 360,000 gallons—of water each year. And Fossil Ridge is 60 percent more energy efficient, saving about $11,500 annually on water alone. If all new school construction and renovations starting today were designed green, energy savings alone would total $20 billion over the next 10 years. But there's more to going green than just dollar signs. With the average school building lasting 42 years, many are aging and beginning to fall apart, says "Building Minds, Minding Buildings," a 2006 report by the American Federation of Teachers. And currently, 14 million kids—more than a quarter of our nation's students—attend schools that are considered substandard or dangerous to their health.

Indeed, a growing number of studies show that a school's physical condition—especially its lighting and indoor air quality—directly affect student performance. "Daylighting in Schools" by the energy efficiency consulting firm Heschong Mahone Group, examined 21,000 students in three elementary school districts in California, Washington, and Colorado and found that kids in classrooms with abundant daylight had up to 25 percent higher learning rates and test scores in reading and math than their peers in rooms with less natural light. A 2005 Turner Construction survey of green buildings found that 70 percent of districts with sustainable schools reported improved student performance. And Global Green USA's Green Schools Report says that standardized test scores dramatically shot up at Charles Young Elementary School in Washington, DC, after it was overhauled in 1997.

It also makes perfect sense that eco-friendly schools affect absenteeism, teacher-retention rates, and health-care costs. One half of our nation's 115,000 schools have problems linked to poor indoor air quality, says Global Green, and since students and teachers spend most of their time indoors, more asthma attacks and respiratory infections mean more sick days.

Edmundson, the principal at Seneca Creek, knows the benefits of going green firsthand. So far, he's had zero teacher turnover, and [in 2006] his students met the state's attendance benchmarks. When it comes to performance, the numbers say it all: 81 percent of his third graders and 87 percent of his fourth graders met or exceeded the state standards for reading, and 77 percent of third graders and 91 percent of fourth graders met the same requirements for math. "Our kids were in the ideal learning environment to succeed," Edmundson says. "There's no way you can have a negative return in this type of environment."

Green Education

For the past 11 years [1996–2007], the nonprofit group Alliance to Save Energy has worked with school districts to train teachers and media specialists in "green education" that adheres to state standards in language arts, science, math, and social studies. And many states, including California, Maryland, and New York, have been extremely receptive, says Swarupa Ganguli, the alliance's senior program manager. The whole point is to "cultivate a whole generation of leaders" who are going to lead environmentally-conscious lives, she says.

School Librarian Karen Kibler at Iroquois High School in Elma, NY, is one of the alliance's most devoted members. She's spent the last decade showing teens how to teach younger students about everything from recycling to remembering to turn off the lights. Up to 30 members of her Energy Saving Club visit local elementary schools each month to lecture about caring for the environment. Her green movement has spread to the rest of the school, with teachers and even the janitorial staff helping to significantly cut waste and bring down electricity bills.

Seneca Creek School Librarian Lisa Norris has also done her share, spending a large part of [2006] helping her central office select wireless tablet computers, energy-efficient flat-screen monitors, and other eco-friendly technology. And she's ordered dozens of print resources, including Angela Royston's *The Life and Times of a Drop of Water*, Chris Van Allsburg's *Just a Dream*, and such classics as Dr. Seuss's *The Lorax*, to help support the school's green focus.

Media specialists are following Kibler's and Norris's lead, taking advantage of the rapidly growing green movement around them. Sandra Latzer of the pre-K–12 Dwight-Englewood School in New Jersey is a key member of her school's green initiative. And Rachel Berkey of Manhattan's Churchill School and Center, a K–12 school for kids with learning disabilities, has made her library as paperless as possible. But when it comes to making environmentally-conscious decisions, there's still one area in which librarians feel helpless—textbook purchases. That's because those decisions are typically made at the district or state level. And although big publishing houses like McGraw-Hill, Scholastic, Penguin, HarperCollins, and Random House now use recycled paper and packaging, the educational textbook market is lagging severely behind, says Erin Johnson, program manager of the Green Press Initiative, an organization that works to preserve endangered forests. The reasons range from the complicated manu-

Financial Benefits of Green Schools	
Financial Benefits of Green Schools	($/ft^2)
Energy	$9
Emissions	$1
Water and Wastewater	$1
Increased Earnings	$49
Asthma Reduction	$3
Cold and Flu Reduction	$5
Teacher Retention	$4
Employment Impact	$2
TOTAL	$74
COST OF GREENING	($3)
NET FINANCIAL BENEFITS	$71

TAKEN FROM: Gregory Kats, "Greening America's Schools: Costs and Benefits," A Capital E Report, http://www.cap-e.com/ewebeditpro/items/059E9819.pdf, October 2006.

facturing process used to make textbooks more durable to the bureaucratic K–12 market. "But it can be done," Johnson says, adding that textbooks and other educational materials represent about 20 percent of the book publishing market, consuming the equivalent of four million trees. That's why her nonprofit group is asking school librarians, teachers, state agencies, and parent-teacher associations to urge those who make textbook purchases to raise this important issue with publishers.

LEED for School

What exactly makes a school green? Words like "green" and "sustainable" simply refer to the things we do to reduce our carbon footprint, or the amount of carbon dioxide emissions we produce. Generally speaking, a green school is one that tries to be as kind to the environment as possible. For example, Cow Hollow preschool in San Francisco, CA, is considered sustainable because it has an active compost heap and community garden, uses green products and pesticides, and incorporates eco-friendly lessons into its curriculum.

Green building, on the other hand, refers to schools like the Sidwell Friends Middle School in Washington, DC, which was specifically designed and constructed to benefit students, teachers, and the environment. Although it's impossible to track the number of schools like Churchill that have adopted green policies, the rising number of LEED-certified schools gives us some idea of just how quickly the movement has taken off. To keep up with the growing trend, in April [2007], USGBC was forced to create an entirely new category called LEED for Schools. Since then, more than 50 new schools have been certified and 400 are registered to become certified, says Rachel Gutter, USGBC's LEED sector manager for K–12 schools. And an additional eight schools are registered for certification under LEED for Existing Buildings.

Before there was a LEED for Schools, there was the Collaborative for High Performance Schools (CHPS), a California-based organization that started in 2000 to help districts in the state design and build green schools. Like USGBC, CHPS offers third-party verification that schools have met the highest performance standards, says Charles Eley, CHPS's executive director.

So far, more than 120 California schools have been built using CHPS's guidelines, including those in the Los Angeles Unified School District, San Diego City Schools, Santa Clara Unified School District, and the Burbank Unified School District. And seven states, including New York, Massachusetts, Vermont, Maine, and New Hampshire, have adopted their own version of CHPS.

Recognizing the benefits of high-performance schools, a growing number of districts and state legislatures are mandating sustainable design for future construction projects. New Jersey public schools requires that all new buildings incorporate LEED guidelines; the Pennsylvania legislature passed a bill to provide financial incentives to public schools that achieve LEED silver certification; and Montgomery County in Maryland passed legislation that requires all county-built or -funded buildings exceeding 10,000 square feet achieve a LEED silver rating. In late 2005, the New York City Council created a set of sustainable standards for public construction projects, making New York the first and largest school district to have green school design, construction, and operation guidelines required by law.

Anne Schopf, a partner at the Seattle-based Mahlum Architects, and the chief designer behind Benjamin Franklin Elementary School in Kirkland, WA, says new state and local requirements to go green have led to a lot of pressure from the top down for school districts to toe the line. And although her firm has upward of 20 ongoing K–12 projects in the pipeline, Schopf says, "It's still an uphill battle" to convince some districts that "you can't afford not to do it."

And she's right. School buildings—an $80 billion industry in 2006–2008—represent the largest construction sector in the country, says USGBC. Yet the cost of constructing a green school only runs about 1.5 percent to 2 percent more than a conventional building, with the payback averaging about two years, says Greg Kats, managing director of Good Energies, a clean-energy venture capital firm, and author of the 2006 report "Greening America's Schools: Costs and Benefits." Building a green school can save $100,000 a year—enough to hire two new teachers, buy 150 new computers, or purchase 5,000 new textbooks, the report says.

Going green is the "right thing" for schools to do, says Kats. Otherwise, "their risk of obsolescence is quite large," he adds. "In five years, every new school is going to be green. So why would anyone want to send their kid to a school that's unhealthy?"

> *"Hospitals are building more efficient, eco-friendly facilities with 'sustainable' design features."*

Hospitals Are Going Green to Cut Toxins

Laura Landro

Laura Landro is a senior editor and writer at the Wall Street Journal, *in which the following viewpoint appeared. She writes that many hospitals are turning to eco-friendly building practices to reduce the amount of toxins in their facilities, which can contribute to longer patient stay and unhealthy working conditions for employees. Landro asserts that while the upfront costs of eco-architecture are higher, the long-term benefits to the environment, the hospital budget, and patients are worth the initial investment.*

As you read, consider the following questions:

1. As of 2006, how many health-care facilities have been built or are being designed, according to the Green Guide to Health Care, as cited by Landro?

2. What benefits have been associated with sustainable health-care facilities, according to the author?

3. Since the mid-1990s, how many medical-waste incinerators have closed, as cited by Landro?

Hospitals play a pivotal role in protecting America's health. But they may also have a surprising unhealthy side— inadvertently contributing to illness and pollution by exposing patients and staff to a witch's brew of toxins from building materials, medical waste, hospital supplies and cleaning products.

Environmental health experts warn that materials that cover floors, walls and ceilings release hundreds of chemicals into hospital air, and chemicals used to clean and maintain hospitals add more. Volatile organic compounds such as formaldehyde, acetaldehyde, naphthalene and toluene are released into the air from particle board, carpets and other finish materials and are inhaled by patients and staff. Polyvinyl chloride (PVC), which releases the carcinogen dioxin during its manufacture, is widely used in the production of IV [intravenous] and blood bags, plastic tubing and other hospital products, as well as carpets.

In addition, inadequate ventilation and generally high energy consumption have contributed to poor air quality and pollution, studies show, with effects ranging from longer patient recovery times to more sick days for staff.

Pressure to Build Green

Now, as the industry embarks on a $200 billion construction program over the next decade to replace or rebuild decaying facilities and meet growing demand from aging baby boomers, that is starting to change. Under pressure from local and state governments, as well as health-care architects and designers and their own environmentally conscious donors, hospitals are building more efficient, eco-friendly facilities with "sustainable" design features that conserve energy, use natural light and materials and reduce potentially dangerous emissions.

About a dozen pioneering groups, including Kaiser Permanente and Dartmouth-Hitchcock Medical Center in Lebanon, N.H., began the move to "green" hospital construction several years ago, and others are now following suit. According to the nonprofit Center for Health Design, which co-sponsored a conference in New Jersey [in September 2006] to promote green design, more than 180 health-care facilities have been built or are being designed and constructed to standards such as those set by the Green Guide for Health Care (GGHC.org), modeled on a certification system developed by the U.S. Green Building Council, a coalition of builders, architects, government agencies and nonprofit groups.

When Kaiser Permanente's new medical center in Modesto, [California,] is completed in 2008, solar panels will cut energy costs, permeable pavement material will filter chemicals from rainwater runoff, floors will be covered with natural rubber, carpets will be backed with recycled safety glass—even toilets will be fitted with special fixtures to conserve water. The new center is part of a $20 billion-plus facilities program at the Oakland, Calif.–based health-care giant that includes building or replacing 27 hospitals over the next nine years.

The Safest Course

To be sure, there is conflicting evidence about the harm caused by chemicals in hospitals, and some manufacturers say there is no direct evidence that PVC, for example, is harmful to humans. But the nonprofit advocacy group Healthcare Without Harm says hospitals have a responsibility to choose the safest course when evidence suggests harmful effects. The group cites studies that show hazardous additives in PVC are toxic to both the reproductive and neurological systems—a particular concern for neonatal-intensive-care patients. The American Hospital Association signed a memorandum of understanding with the Environmental Protection Agency several years ago to phase out the use of mercury, which can affect the human nervous system, in things like thermometers and blood-pressure cuffs.

At the same time, studies show that environmental improvements associated with sustainable buildings, such as bringing in more natural daylight, meditation areas and "healing gardens," can shorten patients' length of stay, reduce reliance on medication, and lessen mental and physical stress.

As hospitals move to make such changes, the challenge now is not only to build hospitals to rigid environmental standards, but also to operate them with the same principles in mind. "You can't build a green hospital and still have Styrofoam cups in the cafeteria," says health-care architect Robin Guenther, a co-coordinator of the Green Guide for Healthcare.

Stiffer federal regulations governing emissions of chemicals and heavy metals like dioxin and mercury have driven some changes, in particular regarding incinerators used to dispose of medical waste. Since the mid 1990s, when regulators found that hospital incinerators were a major contributor to mercury and dioxin emissions, more than 5,000 medical-waste incinerators have closed, and hospitals have adopted safer waste-disposal and treatment technologies.

"Hospitals didn't think of themselves as polluters, with spewing smokestacks and waste going out the back door," says Laura Brannen, executive director of the nonprofit Hospitals for a Healthy Environment (h2e-online.org), which helps hospitals devise improved environmental programs that also shave costs. Among them: separating hazardous waste, infectious waste and solid waste, which must be treated and disposed of differently, and recycling or reclaiming chemicals for medical use.

But Ms. Brannen cautions that many hospitals still send their waste to municipal incinerators that contribute to health threats. Wastewater from hospitals, she adds, still contains toxic lab and cleaning chemicals and pharmaceutical compounds, many of which aren't broken down in sewage-treatment plants.

Choosing Building Materials

Hospitals are also scrambling to find substitutes for building and interior finish materials. And companies that supply the industry are under growing pressure to come up with green products, including latex-free examination gloves, greener cleaners without harsh chemicals and recyclable solvents.

"In an era of rising construction costs, you don't have to pay extra money and use precious health-care dollars just to be green," says Christine Malcolm, Kaiser senior vice president of national facilities and hospitals. With the industry's purchasing power, "we can force suppliers to generate environmentally sensitive products."

Kaiser, for example, pressured carpet manufacturers to come up with a PVC-free product, which it will use in all its new facilities. Kaiser is also installing "dual-flush" toilets, which use more water for flushing solid waste and less for liquid, saving half a gallon of water for the latter. [Since 2001] the company says it has eliminated the purchase and disposal of 40 tons of hazardous chemicals, chosen "ecologically sustainable" materials for 30 million square feet in new construction, and saved more than $10 million a year through energy-conservation strategies.

Saving Money over Time

While many of the innovations cost more up front, they can actually reduce operating costs over time, says Gary Cohen, executive director of the Environmental Health Fund, a non-profit group that works on chemical-safety issues. Rubber flooring is more expensive to install than PVC, for example, "but the hospital will save much more during the lifetime of the flooring due to the fact that you don't need to constantly strip the floor with toxic chemicals and rewax it," Mr. Cohen says.

First, Do No Harm

How buildings are designed, and the materials and methods used to construct and operate them, have significant consequences to the natural environment and health outcomes of people outside of the building envelope as well. Building-related activities are responsible for 35% to 45% of carbon dioxide (CO_2) releases into the atmosphere, a precursor to global warming, and deplete the stratospheric ozone layer by using refrigerants and products, including some insulation materials, manufactured with ozone depleting compounds. Buildings use over 75% of the PVC [polyvinyl chloride] produced. The manufacture and disposal of PVC, as well as its combustion in accidental fires, is linked to the emissions of the persistent and bioaccumulative toxins, dioxins and furans. Construction also accounts for about 40% of raw stone, gravel, sand, and steel consumption, and 25% of virgin wood. Buildings use about 40% of energy resources and 16% of water, while building construction and demolition generates about 25% of municipal solid wastes. Each of these impacts has direct or indirect consequences on human health, the extent of which is becoming better understood as the interconnections between buildings, human health and environmental quality are subjected to more rigorous analyses. . . .

This shift in practice towards green and healthy buildings is fundamentally consistent with the core value of health care professionals—first, do no harm. To this end, healthcare practitioners should assume a public health oriented position relative to the facilities in which they operate, and ensure that these buildings do not degrade the health of individuals or of the general public by implementing sustainable design, operation, and maintenance practices.

Gail Vittori, CleanMed, October 2002.

Still, going green can be challenging for hospitals that have to rebuild or retrofit older facilities. To build the new Lacks Cancer Center, St. Mary's Health in Grand Rapids, Mich., had to tear down old buildings, remove asbestos from pipes, tear out linoleum tiles, and separate metals like steel and copper. But it recycled more than 90 percent of the materials, recrushing brick and cement for the new facility, and installed energy-saving devices like windows with self-cleaning coatings.

"It may have cost us a few dollars more, but in the long run it will pay dividends," says St. Mary's President and Chief Executive Philip H. McCorkle Jr. Another incentive: A local benefactor made a major gift to the hospital contingent on sustainable design. The hospital also prepares food to order, which Mr. McCorkle says uses less energy, wastes less food, and makes patients happier than the traditional cafeteria model.

The University of Pittsburgh Medical Center, which is building a new children's hospital due for completion in 2009, is paying special attention to issues such as materials used to cover and clean floors, since its small patients "are closer to the floors and the source of chemicals," says President and CEO Roger Oxendale. But the hospital is also teaching medical interns about environmental health and reaching out to underserved populations to educate them about issues such as how second-hand smoke can harm their children.

> "The suggestion that the new business
> environmentalism flows simply from a
> heightened concern for the planet is far
> from the truth."

Greenwashing Remains a Challenge to the Green Building Community

Philip Mattera

Philip Mattera is head of the Corporate Research Project, a non-profit center that assists organizations in researching and analyzing companies. In the following viewpoint, he argues that many of the actions taken by large companies are not as beneficial to the environment as they would like consumers to believe. Mattera claims that this type of "greenwashing" is done for good publicity or to protect the companies' bottom lines. Ultimately, he asserts, it is up to environmental activists to lead the way in protecting the planet, not to companies who care only about their profit margins.

Philip Mattera, "The Greenwashing Of America," *TomPaine.com*, June 6, 2007. Copyright © 2007 *TomPaine.com* (A Project of The Institute for America's Future). Reproduced by permission.

As you read, consider the following questions:

1. How much money did Bank of America say it would invest in sustainable projects by 2017, according to Mattera?

2. In the author's opinion, why did people start to question the sincerity of corporate environmentalism in the 1990s?

3. What three possible reasons does Mattera cite for why corporations are not authentically engaged in saving the environment?

In the business world these days, it appears that just about everything is for sale. Multibillion-dollar deals are commonplace, and even venerable institutions such as the *Wall Street Journal* find themselves put into play. Yet companies are not the only things being acquired. This [2007] may turn out to be the year that big business bought a substantial part of the environmental movement.

That's one way of interpreting the remarkable level of cooperation that is emerging between some prominent environmental groups and some of the world's largest corporations. What was once an arena of fierce antagonism has become a veritable love fest as companies profess to be going green and get lavishly honored for doing so. Earlier this year, for instance, the World Resources Institute gave one of its "Courage to Lead" awards to the chief executive of General Electric [GE].

Every day seems to bring another announcement from a large corporation that it is taking steps to protect the planet. IBM, informally known as Big Blue, launched its Project Big Green to help customers slash their data center energy usage. Newmont Mining Co., the world's largest gold digger, endorsed a shareholder resolution calling for a review of its environmental impact. Home Depot introduced an Eco Options label for thousands of green products. General Motors and oil major ConocoPhillips joined the list of corporate giants that have come out in support of a mandatory ceiling on greenhouse gas emissions. Bank of America said it would invest $20 billion in sustainable projects over the next decade.

Many of the new initiatives are being pursued in direct collaboration with environmental groups. Wal-Mart is working closely with Conservation International on its efforts to cut energy usage and switch to renewable sources of power. McDonald's has teamed up with Greenpeace to discourage deforestation caused by the growth of soybean farming in Brazil. When buyout firms Texas Pacific Group and KKR were negotiating the takeover of utility company TXU [in 2007], they asked Environmental Defense to join the talks so that the deal, which ended up including a rollback of plans for 11 new coal-fired plants, could be assured a green seal of approval.

Observing this trend, *Business Week* detects "a remarkable evolution in the dynamic between corporate executives and activists. Once fractious and antagonistic, it has moved toward accommodation and even mutual dependence."

The question is: who is accommodating whom? Are these developments a sign that environmental campaigns have prevailed and are setting the corporate agenda? Or have enviros been duped into endorsing what may be little more than a new wave of corporate greenwash?

An Epiphany About the Environment?

The first thing to keep in mind is that Corporate America's purported embrace of environmental principles is nothing new. Something very similar happened, for example, in early 1990 around the time of the 20th anniversary of Earth Day. *Fortune* announced then that "trend spotters and forward thinkers agree that the Nineties will be the Earth Decade and that environmentalism will be a movement of massive worldwide force." *Business Week* published a story titled "The Greening of Corporate America."

The magazine cited a slew of large companies that were said to be embarking on significant green initiatives, among them DuPont, General Electric, McDonald's, 3M, Union Carbide and Procter & Gamble. Corporations such as these put on their own Earth Tech environmental technology fair on the National Mall and endorsed Earth Day events and promotions.

A difference between then and now is that there was a lot more skepticism about Corporate America's claim of having had an epiphany about the environment. It was obvious to many that business was trying to undo the damage caused by environmental disasters such as Union Carbide's deadly Bhopal [India] chemical leak, the *Exxon Valdez* oil spill in Alaska and the deterioration of the ozone layer. Activist groups charged that corporations were engaging in a bogus public relations effort which they branded "greenwash." Greenpeace staged a protest at DuPont's Earth Tech exhibit, leading to a number of arrests.

Misgivings about corporate environmentalism grew as it was discovered that many of the claims about green products were misleading, false or irrelevant. Mobil Chemical, for instance, was challenged for calling its new Hefty trash bags biodegradable, since that required extended exposure to light rather than their usual fate of being buried in landfills. Procter & Gamble was taken to task for labeling its Pampers and Luvs disposable diapers "compostable" when only a handful of facilities in the entire country were equipped to do such processing. Various companies bragged that their products in aerosol cans were now safe for the environment when all they had done was comply with a ban on the use of chlorofluorocarbons. Some of the self-proclaimed green producers found themselves being investigated by state attorneys general for false advertising and other offenses against the consumer.

Transforming Corporate Images

The insistence that companies actually substantiate their claims put a damper on the entire green product movement. Yet some companies continued to see advantages in being associated with environmental principles. In one of the more brazen moves, DuPont ran TV ads in the late 1990s depicting sea lions applauding a passing oil tanker (accompanied by Beethoven's "Ode to Joy") to take credit for the fact that its Conoco subsidiary had begun using double hulls in its ships, conveniently failing to mention that it was one of the last oil companies to take that step.

At the same time, some companies began to infiltrate the environmental movement itself by contributing to the more moderate groups and getting spots on their boards. They also joined organizations such as CERES, which encourages green groups and corporations to endorse a common set of principles. By the early 2000s, some companies sought to depict themselves as being not merely in step with the environmental movement but at the forefront of a green transformation. British Petroleum [BP] started publicizing its investments in renewable energy and saying that its initials really stood for Beyond Petroleum—all despite the fact that its operations continued to be dominated by fossil fuels.

This paved the way for General Electric's "ecomagination" p.r. [public relations] blitz, which it pursued even while dragging its feet in the cleanup of PCB contamination in New York's Hudson River. GE was followed by Wal-Mart, which in October 2005 sought to transform its image as a leading cause of pollution-generating sprawl by announcing a program to move toward zero waste and maximum use of renewable energy. In recent months the floodgates have opened, with more and more large companies calling for federal caps on greenhouse gas emissions. In January [2007] ten major corporations—including Alcoa, Caterpillar, DuPont and General Electric—joined with the Natural Resources Defense Council and

Rules of Thumb for Detecting Greenwashing

Big budget greenwash campaigns are designed to defuse skepticism of journalists, politicians and activists. Some rough rules of thumb for testing whether the claims made by a company, government or NGO [nongovernmental organization] stack up are:

Follow the money trail: many companies are donors to political parties, think tanks and other groups in the community. . . .

Follow the membership trail: Many companies boast about the virtues of their environmental policy and performance but hide their anti-environmental activism behind the banner of an industry association to which they belong. . . .

Test for international consistency: Most companies will operate to different standards in other countries.

Test for consistency over time: It is common for a company to launch a policy or initiative and then starve it of funds. Or a company will make promises when they are under public pressure but never implement them when the spotlight fades.

"Greenwashing," SourceWatch, *2007.*

other enviro groups in forming the U.S. Climate Action Partnership. A few months later, General Motors, arguably one of the companies that has done the most to exacerbate global warming, signed on as well.

A Cause for Celebration or Dismay?

Today the term "greenwash" is rarely uttered, and differences in positions between corporate giants and mainstream environmental groups are increasingly difficult to discern. Everywhere one looks, enviros and executives have locked arms and are marching together to save the planet. Is this a cause for celebration or dismay?

Answering this question begins with the recognition that companies do not all enter the environmental fold in the same way. Here are some of their different paths:

- Defeat. Some companies did not embrace green principles on their own—they were forced to do so after being successfully targeted by aggressive environmental campaigns. Home Depot abandoned the sale of lumber harvested in old-growth forests several years ago after being pummeled by groups such as Rainforest Action Network. Responding to similar campaign pressure, Boise Cascade also agreed to stop sourcing from endangered forests and J.P. Morgan Chase agreed to take environmental impacts into account in its international lending activities. Dell started taking computer recycling seriously only after it was pressed to do so by groups such as the Silicon Valley Toxics Coalition.

- Diversion. It is apparent that Wal-Mart is using its newfound green consciousness as a means of diverting public attention away from its dismal record in other areas, especially the treatment of workers. In doing so, it hopes to peel environmentalists away from the broad anti-Wal-Mart movement. BP's emphasis on the environment was no doubt made more urgent by the need to repair an image damaged by allegations that a 2005 refinery fire in Texas that killed 15 people was the fault of management. To varying degrees, many other companies that have jumped on the green bandwagon have sins they want the public to forget.

- Opportunism. There is so much hype these days about protecting the environment that many companies are going green simply to earn more green. There are some market moves, such as Toyota's push on hybrids, that also appear to have some environmental legitimacy. Yet there are also instances of sheer opportunism, such as the effort by Nuclear Energy Institute to depict nukes as an environmentally desirable alternative to fossil fuels. Not to mention surreal cases such as the decision by Britain's BAE Systems to develop environmentally friendly munitions, including low-toxin rockets and lead-free bullets.

In other words, the suggestion that the new business environmentalism flows simply from a heightened concern for the planet is far from the truth. Corporations always act in their own self-interest and one way or another are always seeking to maximize profits. It used to be that they had to hide that fact. Today they flaunt it, because there is a widespread notion that eco-friendly policies are totally consistent with cutting costs and fattening the bottom line.

When GE's "ecomagination" campaign was launched, CEO Jeffrey Immelt insisted "it's no longer a zero-sum game—things that are good for the environment are also good for business." This was echoed by Wal-Mart CEO Lee Scott, who said in a speech announcing his company's green initiative that "being a good steward of the environment and in our communities, and being an efficient and profitable business, are not mutually exclusive. In fact they are one [and] the same." That's probably because Scott sees environmentalism as merely an extension of the company's legendary penny-pinching, as glorified efficiency measures.

Chevron Wants to Lead

Many environmental activists seem to welcome the notion of a convergence of business interests and green interests, but it all seems too good to be true. If eco-friendly policies are entirely "win-win," then why did corporations resist them for so long? It is hard to believe that the conflict between profit maximization and environmental protection, which characterized the entire history of the ecological movement, has suddenly evaporated.

Either corporations are fooling themselves, in which case they will eventually realize there is no environmental free lunch and renege on their green promises. Or they are fooling us and are perpetrating a massive public relations hoax. A third interpretation is that companies are taking voluntary steps that are genuine but inadequate to solve the problems at hand and are mainly meant to prevent stricter, enforceable regulation.

In any event, it would behoove enviros to be more skeptical of corporate green claims and less eager to jump into bed with business. It certainly makes sense to seek specific concessions from corporations and to offer moderate praise when they comply, but activists should maintain an arm's-length relationship to business and not see themselves as partners. After all, the real purpose of the environmental movement is not simply to make technical adjustments to the way business operates (that's the job of consultants) but rather to push for fundamental and systemic changes.

Moreover, there is a risk that the heightened level of collaboration will undermine the justification for an independent environmental movement. Why pay dues to a green group if its agenda is virtually identical to that of GE and DuPont? Already there are hints that business views itself, not activist groups, as the real green vanguard. Chevron, for instance, has been running a series of environmental ads with the tagline "Will you join us?"

Join them? Wasn't it Chevron and the other oil giants that played a major role in creating global warming? Wasn't it Chevron that used the repressive regime in Nigeria to protect its environmentally destructive operations in the Niger Delta? Wasn't it Chevron's Texaco unit that dumped more than 18 billion gallons of toxic waste in Ecuador? And wasn't it Chevron that was accused of systematically underpaying royalties to the federal government for natural gas extracted from the Gulf of Mexico? That is not the kind of track record that confers the mantle of environmental leadership.

In fact, we shouldn't be joining any company's environmental initiative. Human activists should be leading the effort to clean up the planet, and corporations should be made to follow our lead.

> *"Though extreme eco-architecture may not be a solution to a thoroughly sustainable building industry, it certainly provides an ideal."*

Ephemeral Structures Are the Ideal Eco-Architecture

Jo Scheer

Jo Scheer is a builder and designer and the author of Building with Bamboo. *In the following viewpoint, he recommends that home builders interested in eco-friendly practices should consider ephemeral architecture—easily transportable structures that use very little resources to build and maintain. To that end, he constructed a hooch, which is basically a free-standing tree house. Although he acknowledges that the hooch and other types of ephemeral structures are a type of extreme eco-design, he thinks that they are particularly well suited for the way human beings live.*

As you read, consider the following questions:

1. What is extreme eco-design, according to Scheer?

2. What does the author say biomimicry is?

Jo Scheer, "The Hooch: An Extreme Eco-structure," *EcoBuilding Times*, Fall 2005. www.ecobuilding.org/green_building/newsletter_PDFs/newsletter_Fall2005.pdf. Reproduced by permission of the author.

3. From what source does Speer say the name *hooch* is derived?

Today's architecture of single-family new construction seems to be diverging into two distinct trends—at very opposite ends of the spectrum. No longer built are the modest, post W[orld] W[ar] II single-family homes that many of us grew up in. Instead we are seeing the rise of McMansions, starter-castles, monster houses, or mega-homes. The total disregard for adhering to the architectural style in older neighborhoods in pursuit of a statement of individual wealth, expressed in terms of house size, is perceived by many as just plain rude. The generally abhorred McMansion has somehow become a demanded trend and has reached the point of inducing municipal regulations limiting the percentage of lot size that can be devoted to building.

The newly immerging hot ticket, though not nearly as prevalent as McMansions, is the building of eco-conscious, sustainable housing, also known as "green" homes. With an all-encompassing philosophy of earth friendliness, these homes incorporate everything from recycled materials to renewable energy. The philosophy and design can add significantly to overall first costs, but savings over time and an increasing demand are bringing prices down. These "eco homes" may have the best of intentions but are often difficult to assess in terms of energy efficiency and eventual payback of these first costs. As every building is designed specifically for the site and climate, the prediction of energy use can only be a reasonable approximation, subject to a myriad of factors.

A third alternative, albeit a radical approach, is the adaptation of a philosophy of extreme eco-design embracing efficient material use, minimal site impact, energy efficiency, biomimetics, ephemerals, and lifestyle. Extreme eco-design takes the philosophy of earth friendliness to the ultimate degree, the most efficient and most earth friendly possible design that can be achieved.

Efficient material use can be achieved in many ways. Recycling materials from existing structures or teardowns is efficient in material use, but can be time consuming and labor intensive, and is subject to availability. It is an approach that can add character and charm through the reuse of materials that would otherwise be too expensive or otherwise unobtainable today and is thereby construed as cost-effective. Another approach is to just simply use less. A smaller, less complicated dwelling with an open floor plan, can reduce material use significantly.

Site alteration, whether intentional or unintentional, has many implications. Denuding of vegetation, and the consequential erosion and run-off, is not earth friendly. If a site is selected for its proximity to nature, the despoiling of the site is indeed counter-productive. Pre-fabrication can preclude the necessity of massive site alteration, as the whole structure can be fabricated elsewhere, and quickly assembled on site. Ideally, however, a design that utilizes a philosophy of a small [environmental] footprint is the most effective strategy. It can expand the possible locations for a building, and allow a building to fit into its surroundings.

Ephemeral Structures

Taking this to the extreme, why have any foundation at all? Ephemerals in architecture are somewhat radical, but not illogical. Our time on this earth is ephemeral, temporary. To protect us from the elements, a shelter or structure does not need to last for millennia. It is merely an extension of our brief existence. Smaller, lighter, and with a figurative and literal small footprint, the ephemeral structure embodies the epitome of earth friendliness. As a temporary structure, the additional cost and disruption of the site with a permanent foundation is avoided. The ephemeral shelter sits on a minimal, floating, temporary foundation. And, as a mobile creature, this shelter can easily be dismantled and moved.

Micro-Compact Homes

Welcome to the micro-compact home. The m-ch, for short, is a 76-square-foot domicile designed by Technical University of Munich professor Richard Horden to meet the growing demand for short-stay living.

And this isn't just a dressed-up shack; the m-ch is the BMW of small homes. For $96,000 a cube (including delivery and installation anywhere in Europe), owners get a fully integrated interior teched out with everything from a flatscreen TV to a dining room table that seats five. In the future, solar panels and a roof-mounted horizontal-axis wind turbine generating 2,200 kilowatts of power a year will make m-ch models self-sustaining.

The concept and philosophy of a small footprint can be seen in nature. A single trunk, securely anchored with an extensive root system, supports the giant canopy of a tree. As a model, there can be no better source than nature. The architecture of plants today is the culmination of millions of years of evolution—and only the successful strategies surround us today. Biomimicry, or the imitation of strategies of the natural world, has become a fundamental tenet of good design, and a driving force of innovation.

Clearly, the most pervasive element promoting this extreme eco-structure model is lifestyle. A mobile, free, and non-materialistic individual is an ideal, not a reality. It is an imaginary model born of the stark realities of modern life—stable, family-oriented, career-minded existences in established, mortgaged homes. Yet, the desire, and ideal, still exists.

Perhaps a niche for this small, ephemeral, pre-fabricated, eco-friendly, and escapist structural ideal exists as well.

The Hooch

One such structure that adheres to all the criteria of the extreme eco-structure is the hooch—a concept and reality for a select group of my clients and myself. The hooch, (the name derives from the Japanese word "uchi", meaning dwelling) has become a fun, though minor enterprise since the original hooch was built in 1997—as the master bedroom of our home in Puerto Rico. Originally designed to utilize and exploit the structural qualities of bamboo, it proved itself worthy, after surviving intact a category three hurricane—winds greater than 120 mph.

The flexibility of the bamboo, and the resiliency of the design, was vindicated in one, awesome night. A move to a rented home in Ashland [Oregon] prompted a unanimous family nostalgia for the hooch—a place that we all enjoyed. The ephemeral, small footprint hooch was born in concept, and reality, in our backyard. Pre-fabricated, supported on a single point foundation, and balanced with cables to the surrounding trees, the new hooch soon hosted sleep-outs and parties with an occupancy rate requiring family member reservations a week in advance. The design was documented, and subsequent hooches have been built from L.A. to Eugene [Oregon].

The ephemeral quality of the hooch was demonstrated [in 2004], upon purchasing our new home. The hooch was dismantled, moved, and re-assembled in our new backyard in a matter of days. It stands in a grove of Douglas fir trees, with a killer view of Mt. Ashland. The hooch continues to serve as the master bedroom, as the parents sleep out 9 months of the year. Kid sleep outs, parties, and occasional daytime respites from the box on the ground (our mortgaged house) verify its utility, and add a mystical, adventurous quality to our backyard escapes.

Other hooches enjoy sites much more exotic—the banks of the Long Tom River in Eugene, overlooking a man-made pond in a canyon in Sonoma County [California], and our new, completely self-sufficient hooch—with another killer view of the Caribbean ocean. Equipped with a 12-volt solar photovoltaic, solar hot water, a full kitchenette, and a "hoochette" bathroom with flush toilet, the new hooch was the culmination of a desire to build the ultimate eco-structure. The crowning achievement is the use of bamboo poles harvested from our very own bamboo groves, planted by myself. The fast growing and renewable nature of bamboo is demonstrated in an eco-friendly hooch. Now, more than a year later, I have an even greater inventory of bamboo for more hooches, to support my eccentricity.

Though extreme eco-architecture may not be a solution to a thoroughly sustainable building industry, it certainly provides an ideal. It is a model of ideas and concepts that beg to be assimilated. The hooch is merely an example of where the philosophy can lead, though for those lucky enough to experience it, the hooch becomes an integral/necessary part of their existence. Rise above it all, in a hooch.

Periodical Bibliography

The following articles have been selected to supplement the diverse views presented in this chapter.

Joan Blumenfeld   "Green Distinction Changing Texture of Interior Design," *Real Estate Weekly*, June 20, 2007.

Goldie Blumenstyk   "Is College Landscaping Green Enough?" *Chronicle of Higher Education*, October 12, 2007.

Indoor Environment Quality Strategies   "Army Moving to LEED," September 2006.

Raj Jadhav   "Green Architecture in India," *UN Chronicle*, June 2006.

Steven Litt   "The Greening of Museum Architecture," *ARTnews*, October 2007.

Nicolai Ouroussoff   "Why Are They Greener than We Are?" *New York Times Magazine*, May 20, 2007.

Joetta Sack-Min   "Districts Reap Cost Savings by Building 'Green Schools,'" *Education Digest*, October 2007.

Ted Shelton   "Greening the White House," *Journal of Architectural Education*, May 2007.

Josh Sims   "Eco-Clubbing Is Coming," *Independent* (London), May 31, 2007.

Debra Lau Whelan   "School Libraries Join Green Movement," *School Library Journal*, July 2007.

For Further Discussion

Chapter 1

1. Bion Howard discusses the main features of green homes and communities. How have the other viewpoints in this chapter shaped your ideas about what it means to build green?

2. Rod F. Wille argues that eco-architecture is good for business, while Frank Musica warns that building green can be costly to designers. How does each viewpoint influence your understanding of the issue?

3. What evidence does Stephen del Percio offer to support his argument that building conditions can make workers sick? What evidence do Alexi Marmot et al. offer to support that stress is actually the main cause of employee illnesses? Whose viewpoint do you find more convincing, and why?

Chapter 2

1. An interviewee in the Jeffrey Kaye viewpoint argues that eco-architecture helps the environment. Jane Powell argues that eco-architecture might help the environment somewhat but that its benefits are exaggerated by proponents. After reading these two viewpoints, what effect do you think eco-architecture has on the environment? Why?

2. Stan Cox argues that large houses cannot be eco-friendly while the article by Claire Anderson suggests that they can. Which viewpoint offers the strongest evidence? Explain your answer.

3. Carl Pope and Randall G. Holcombe debate the alternatives for curbing urban sprawl. Which viewpoint is more convincing? Why?

Chapter 3

1. Patrick W. Rollens argues that it is becoming easier to build green. Auden Schendler argues that green building remains challenging. Based on the evidence offered, do you think it is still difficult to employ sustainable building techniques? Why or why not?

2. Alanna Stang and Christopher Hawthorne argue that eco-architecture is no longer unattractive, while Stan Cox argues that homeowners associations continue to ban green building implementations such as solar panels. After reading these viewpoints, do you think home owners should be allowed to use eco-friendly features on their property? Defend your answer.

3. What evidence does Taryn Holowka use to argue that the Leadership in Energy and Environmental Design (LEED) guidelines help builders build green? What evidence does Ted Smalley Bowen use to argue that LEED's effectiveness is dubious? Whose viewpoint is more convincing to you, and why?

Chapter 4

1. Timothy Egan and Debra Lau Whelan discuss efforts among colleges and high schools to go green, and Laura Landro explains why hospitals are doing the same. What are the benefits of employing eco-architecture practices in these environments? Can you imagine any objections to implementing eco-friendly building practices at schools and/or hospitals?

2. Philip Mattera argues that greenwashing continues to plague the green building industry. In what ways might greenwashing be eliminated?

3. Jo Scheer describes the hooch, a type of ephemeral architecture. What are the benefits and limitations of such a structure? Would you live in one? Why or why not?

Organizations to Contact

The editors have compiled the following list of organizations concerned with the issues debated in this book. The descriptions are derived from materials provided by the organizations. All have publications or information available for interested readers. The list was compiled on the date of publication of the present volume; the information provided here may change. Be aware that many organizations take several weeks or longer to respond to inquiries, so allow as much time as possible.

Alliance to Save Energy

1850 M St. NW, Suite 600, Washington, DC   20036
(202) 857-0666 • fax: (202) 331-9588
e-mail: info@ase.org
Web site: www.ase.org

Founded in 1977, the Alliance to Save Energy is a nonprofit coalition of business, government, environmental and consumer leaders that supports energy efficiency as a cost-effective energy resource and advocates energy-efficiency policies. To carry out its mission, the Alliance to Save Energy undertakes research, educational programs, and policy advocacy, designs and implements energy-efficiency projects, promotes technology development and deployment, and builds public-private partnerships, in the United States and other countries. In addition to a regular e-newsletter, the alliance Web site features a number of research and position papers, including "Energy Efficiency Potential in American Buildings" and "Conservation Is Not a Four-Letter Word."

American Society of Heating, Refrigerating, and Air Conditioning Engineers (ASHRAE)

1791 Tullie Cir. NE, Atlanta, GA   30329
(800)527-4723 • fax: (404) 321-5478

e-mail: ashrae@ashrae.org
Web site: www.ashrae.org

Founded in 1894, ASHRAE is an international organization that works to advance heating, ventilation, air conditioning, and refrigeration to serve humanity and promote a sustainable world through research, standards writing, publishing, and continuing education. In addition to a national conference, ASHRAE regularly publishes position papers, the *ASHRAE Journal, ASHRAE Insights*, and several newsletters. Some of the publications available on its Web site include "Climate Change" and "Building Sustainability."

EnergyStar Program
1200 Pennsylvania Ave. NW, Washington, DC   20460
(888)782-7937
Web site: energystar.gov

In 1992 the U.S. Environmental Protection Agency (EPA) introduced EnergyStar as a voluntary labeling program designed to identify and promote energy-efficient products to reduce greenhouse gas emissions. In 1996, EPA partnered with the U.S. Department of Energy, and the EnergyStar label is now on major appliances, office equipment, lighting, home electronics, and more in new homes and commercial and industrial buildings. In addition to annual reports and regular podcasts, the EnergyStar Web site offers a number of publications, including energy-saving advisory reports, guidelines for new homes, and checklists for home improvements.

Environmental News Network (ENN)
402 N. B St., Fairfield, IA   52556
(800) 957-8599 • fax: (641) 472-2790
Web site: www.enn.com

Since 1993, ENN has been educating the world about environmental issues. Its Web site offers environmental news, live chats, daily feature stories, forums for debate, audio, video, and more in an effort to provide unbiased information about current environmental debates. Some recent ENN publications have focused on ocean pollution, Spain's sustainability policies, and the connection between the demise of coral reefs and automobile emissions.

Healthy Building Network (HBN)

Institute for Local Self-Reliance, 1313 Fifth St. SE
Minneapolis, MN   55414
(612) 379-3815 • fax: (612) 379-3920
e-mail: info@healthybuilding.net
Web site: www.healthybuilding.net

HBN is a national network of green building professionals, environmental and health activists, socially responsible investment advocates, and others who are interested in promoting healthier building materials as a means of improving public health and preserving the global environment. Specifically, HBN focuses on the elimination of polyvinyl chloride (PVC) plastics, plywood and chipboards, formaldehyde, and wood treated with copper chromium arsenate in new and refurbished construction. In addition to *Healthy Building News*, a weekly e-newsletter, HBN regularly publishes research and position statements, such as "Green Communities: A Partnership Between the Enterprise Foundation and the Natural Resources Defense Council" and "Life Cycle Analysis and Green Building: Credibility at the Crossroads."

Environmental Protection Agency (EPA)

1200 Pennsylvania Ave. NW, Washington, DC   20460
(202) 343-9370 • fax: (202) 343-2394
Web site: www.epa.gov

Since 1970, the EPA has been working for cleaner, healthier water, land, and air to protect human health and the environment. The EPA works to develop and enforce regulations that implement environmental laws enacted by Congress. The EPA is responsible for researching and setting national standards for a variety of environmental programs and delegates to states the responsibility for issuing permits and for monitoring and enforcing compliance. In addition to maintaining a database of environmentally related hotlines and clearinghouses, the EPA offers a number of online publications, including "Air Quality and Emissions Trends Report" and *Healthy Buildings, Healthy People: A Vision for the 21st Century.*

Smart Growth America (SGA)

1707 L St NW, Suite 1050, Washington, DC   20036
(202) 207-3355 • fax: (202) 207-3349
e-mail: sga@smartgrowthamerica.org
Web site: http://smartgrowthamerica.org

SGA is a coalition of national, state, and local organizations working to improve the ways that cities and towns are planned. The coalition includes many national organizations advocating on behalf of historic preservation, the environment, farmland and open-space preservation, and neighborhood revitalization. The SGA Web site offers a number of resources, including such publications as "Growing Cooler: The Evidence on Urban Development and Climate Change" and "Vacant Properties: The True Cost to Communities."

Sustainable Buildings Industry Council (SBIC)

1112 Sixteenth St. NW, Suite 240, Washington, DC   20036
(202) 628-7400 • fax: (202) 393-5043
e-mail: sbic@sbicouncil.org
Web site: www.sbicouncil.org

Since 1980, SBIC has been an association of building associations committed to high-performance design and construction in conjunction with the fields of architecture, engineering, building systems and materials, product manufacturing, energy analysis, and "whole building" design. In addition to providing online tools for building industry professionals, SBIC also publishes reports about sustainable building practices. Some of SBIC's publications include *Green Building Guidelines: Meeting the Demand for Low-Energy, Resource-Efficient Homes and High-Performance School Buildings Resource and Strategy Guide.*

United Nations Division for Sustainable Development (UNDSD)
Two United Nations Plaza, Rm. DC2-2220
New York, NY   10017
(212) 963-8102 • fax: (212) 963-4260
Web site: www.un.org/esa/sustdev/

The UN Division for Sustainable Development provides leadership and is an authoritative source of expertise within the United Nations system on sustainable development. The UNDSD maintains a database of world statistics on sustainability and a collection of news reports on current sustainable activities in world nations. In addition to position statements and FAQ sheets, the UNDSD Web site offers a number of other publications, including *Trends in Sustainable Development and Sustainable Consumption* and *Production: Promoting Climate-Friendly Household Consumption Patterns.*

United States Green Building Council (USGBC)
1015 Eighteenth St. NW, Suite 805, Washington, DC   20036
(202) 828-7422 • fax: (202) 828-5110
e-mail: info@usgbc.org
Web site: www.usgbc.org

USGBC is a nonprofit organization composed of more than twelve thousand organizations from across the building industry that are working to advance structures that are environmentally responsible, profitable, and healthy places to live and work. USGBC's major effort is LEED (Leadership in Energy and Environmental Design), a voluntary, consensus-based national rating system for developing high-performance, sustainable buildings. USGBC offers online courses and other educational materials, including a number of publications, such as *GreenSource* and "A National Green Building Research Agenda."

World Green Building Council (WGBC)
110 Sutter St., Suite 712, San Francisco, CA   94104
(415) 352-5200 • fax: (415) 352-5210

e-mail: info@worldgbc.org
Web site: www.worldgbc.org

WGBC is a union of national councils whose mission is to accelerate the transformation of the global property industry towards sustainability. Since 1999 WGBC has served as the main voice for the green building councils that it represents and has supported the development and use of green building rating systems, such as LEED and EnergyStar. In addition to worldwide sustainable building case studies, the WGBC Web site offers a number of publications, including the *World Green Building Council Newsletter* and *The Dollars and Sense of Green Buildings.*

Bibliography of Books

Ian Abley and Jonathan Schwinge
Manmade Modular Megastructures. Chichester, UK: Wiley-Academy, 2005.

Claus Bech-Danielsen
Ecological Reflections in Architecture: Architectural Design of the Place, the Space and the Interface. Copenhagen: Danish Architectural Press, 2005.

Geoffrey Broadbent and C.A. Brebbia, eds.
Eco-Architecture: Harmonisation Between Architecture and Nature. Ashurst, UK: WIT, 2006.

Sandra Leibowitz Earley
Ecological Design and Building Schools: Green Guide to Educational Opportunities in the United States and Canada. Oakland, CA: New Village, 2005.

Brian Edwards
Rough Guide to Sustainability. London: RIBA, 2002.

Kari Foster, Annette Stelmack, and Debbie Hindman
Sustainable Residential Interiors. Hoboken, NJ: Wiley, 2007.

Warwick Fox, ed.
Ethics and the Built Environment. New York: Routledge, 2000.

Simon Guy and Steven Moore
Sustainable Architectures: Cultures and Natures in Europe and North America. New York: Spon, 2005.

Takahiko
Hasegawa

Environmentally Sustainable Buildings: Challenges and Policies. Paris: OECD, 2003.

Richard Hyde
et al.

The Environmental Brief: Pathways for Green Design. New York: Taylor and Francis, 2007.

Lal Jayamaha

Energy-Efficient Building Systems: Green Strategies for Operation and Maintenance. New York: McGraw-Hill, 2007.

Stephen R. Kellert

Building for Life: Designing and Understanding the Human-Nature Connection. Washington, DC: Island, 2005.

Ralph L. Knowles

Ritual House: Drawing on Nature's Rhythms for Architecture and Urban Design. Washington, DC: Island, 2006.

Alison G. Kwok
and Walter T.
Grondzik

The Green Studio Handbook: Environmental Strategies for Schematic Design. Burlington, MA: Architectural, 2007.

C.J Lim and
Ed Liu, eds.

How Green Is Your Garden? London: Wiley-Academy, 2003.

Jason F.
McLennan

The Philosophy of Sustainable Design: The Future of Architecture. Kansas City, MO: Ecotone, 2004.

Sandra Mendler,
William Odell,
and Mary Ann
Lazarus

The HOK Guidebook to Sustainable Design. 2nd ed. Hoboken, NJ: Wiley, 2006.

Arian Mostaedi	*Sustainable Architecture: Lowtech Houses*. Barcelona, Spain: Carlos Boto i Comera, 2002.
David Pearson	*In Search of Natural Architecture*. London: Gaia, 2005.
William G. Ramroth Jr.	*Planning for Disaster: How Natural and Man-Made Disasters Shape the Built Environment*. New York: Kaplan, 2007.
Amos Rapoport	*Culture, Architecture, and Design*. Chicago: Locke Science, 2005.
Sue Roaf, Manuel Fuentes and Stephanie Thomas	*Ecohouse: A Design Guide*. Boston: Elsevier/Architectural, 2007.
Susan Roaf	*Closing the Loop: Benchmarks for Sustainable Buildings*. London: RIBA, 2004.
Jennifer Roberts	*Good Green Homes*. Salt Lake City: Gibbs Smith, 2003.
Jeannie Leggett Sikora	*Profit from Building Green: Award Winning Tips to Build Energy Efficient Homes*. Washington, DC: BuilderBooks, 2002.
Peter F. Smith	*Architecture in a Climate of Change: A Guide to Sustainable Design*. Boston: Elsevier/Architectural, 2005.

Clarke Snell and Tim Callahan

Building Green: A Complete How-to Guide to Alternative Building Methods: Earth Plaster, Straw Bale, Cordwood, Cob, Living Roofs. New York: Lark, 2005.

Catherine Spellman, ed.

Re-envisioning Landscape/Architecture. Barcelona, Spain: Actar, 2003.

James Steele

Ecological Architecture: A Critical History. London: Thames and Hudson, 2005.

Bill Streever

Green Seduction: Money, Business, and the Environment. Jackson: University Press of Mississippi, 2007.

Randall Thomas, ed.

Environmental Design: An Introduction for Architects and Engineers. New York: Taylor and Francis, 2006.

Sim Van der Ryn

Design for Life: The Architecture of Sim Van der Ryn. Salt Lake City: Gibbs Smith, 2005.

Ken Yeang

Ecodesign: A Manual for Ecological Design. Hoboken, NJ: Wiley, 2006.

Index

A

Accredited Professional (AP), 154
Acid rain, 65
Active materials, green homes, 23
Affordability, housing, 30–32, 98
Air circulation, straw bale home, 87
Air quality/pollution, indoor
  buildings, 65
  filters, 27–28
  green schools, 180
  hospitals, 187
  indoor *vs.* outdoor, 148
  test kits, 27
  See also Indoor air quality; Pollution
Alberici Enterprises, 118
Allergies, air filtration, 27–28, 48
Alliance to Save Energy, 181
American Chemistry Council, 92
American Federation of Teachers, 180
American Hospital Association, 188
American Lung Association, 29
American Society of Heating, Refrigerating and Air-Conditioning Engineers (ASHRAE), 49
Anderson, Claire, 78–88
Anderson, Ray, 121
AP. *See* Accredited Professional
Architects, green buildings, 67–68
Architectural review committee, 139
Arizona State University, 230
Automobile pollution, 24, 28, 32

B

Barlett, Peggy F., 173
Bead board, reclaimed, 86
Beria College, 171
Bernick, Michael, 62
Biomimicry, 125–126, 206
Bowen, Ted Smalley, 155–164
Brannen, Laura, 189
Brewery Lofts, 135
BRI. *See* building related illness (BRI)
British Petroleum (BP), 197
Brooks, Angela, 132–133
Brown, Elizabeth Cady, 167
Brown, Michael, 126
Building related illness (BRI), 50
Buildings, commercial/residential
  eco-architecture, 34
  energy efficiency, 204
  environmental impact/benefits, 65, 67, 76
  first cost *vs.* life cycle cost, 116–117
  hospital materials, 190
  integrated, 35–36
  LEED, 149–150, 158
  management considerations, 59
  recycling material, 73
  residential design, 131–132
  resource usage, 47
  SBS, 53
  site considerations, 29–30, 205
  size restriction, 76
Burritt Museum, 81

C

California Sustainable Building Task Force, 117

California Title 24 energy code, 39, 73

Carbon dioxide
  building generated, 65, 191
  concrete, 91
  green building, 128, 183
  SBS, 48, 54
  wood, 92

Carlson, Richard, 135–136

Carnegie Mellon University, 171, 175–177

Cashman, Doug, 83

Centers for Disease Control and Prevention (CDC), 19

Cervero, Robert, 62

CFLs. *See* Compact fluorescent bulbs

Charles Young Elementary School, 181

Chase, Geoffrey W., 173

Chevron Oil Company, 200–202

Christie, Les, 95

City Limits Magazine, 167

Clements, Jonathan, 93–94

Clotheslines, restrictions, 140–142

CNNMoney.com, 95

Coal, 65, 195

Coburn, Deborah, 134

College campuses, as eco-friendly
  green credentials, 170
  living roof, 171, 174
  student involvement, 173
  sustainability, 171–172

Colorado Court, 132

Commercial buildings. *See* buildings, commercial/residential

Commercial development, 98–99

Community ties, 30–32

Commuting, 31, 102

Compact fluorescent bulbs (CFLs), 73–74

Competing programs, LEED, 160

Concrete, manufacture/transportation of, 91

Conservation Law Foundation (CLF), 158

Consumer Product Safety Commission (CPSC), 28

Corporate leadership, green building, 125

Corporate profits, 77

The Corporation (documentary), 121

Costs
  conventional construction, 148
  eco-architecture recovery, 34–35, 42–44
  first *vs.* life cycle, 116–117
  green building, 30–32, 69, 113, 120, 125
  infrastructure, 31, 98
  leapfrog development, 99
  LEED, 148, 157
  social reductions, 42
  square footage, 117
  urban sprawl, 99, 105–106
  zero net effective increase, 117

Cox, Stan, 89–96, 137–146

CPSC. *See* Consumer Product Safety Commission

Crime rate, planned communities, 32

Cultural/structural resistance, green building, 125

Culver, Katey, 82

D

Davidson, Cliff, 176

Davis Langdon (consulting company), 120

De Havillan, Joanne, 81

Decentralization, 102–103, 109–110

Del Percio, Stephen, 46–51

Design professional, risk to, 42–43

Deutsch, Randy, 116–117

Diamond, Mary, 79

DiMassa, Cara Mia, 63

Double-pane doors/windows, 87

Drury University, 172

Dual flush fixtures, 34–35

Dwight-Englewood School, 182

E

Earth Day, 138

Eastgate Building, 126–127

Eco-architecture, aesthetic increases in
eco-banality, 130
green design *vs.* academic architecture, 130–131
low-income housing, 132–133
recycled materials, 136
residential design, 131–132
solar panels, 132–133, 134
sustainability, 131

Eco-architecture, as business benefit
building types, 34
cost recovery, 34–35
dual flush fixtures, 34–35
as economic investment, 34
heliostat deflecting mirrors, 36
integrated design, 35–36
LEED guideline utilization, 37
low VOC paint, 36
natural daylight, 36–37
photovoltaic panels, 35
specialized products, 36–37
sunshade prisms, 36
sustainable design advantages, 38

Eco-architecture, as business risk
cost recovery, 43–44

design professional risk, 42–43
designers *vs.* owners, 41–42
expectations, 43
fraud/misrepresentation claims, 45
implied/express warranties, 44–45
LEED rating system, 41
liability exposure, 40, 42–45
manufacturers warranties, 43
social cost reductions, 42
sustainable design standards, 40–41

Eco-architecture, environmental help for
acid rain, 65
air pollution, buildings, 65
architects, 67–68
carbon dioxide, 65
coal mining, 65
electricity consumption, 65
energy use, buildings *vs.* cars/trucks, 65
environmental impact, 65, 67, 76
government support, 68–69
gray-water, 67
green building effectiveness, 66
resistance to, 69–70
sulfur dioxide, 65

Eco-banality, 130

Eco-Manor, 86

The Ecology of Commerce (Hawken), 121

Economic cost, urban sprawl, 105–106

Egan, Timothy, 169–177

Eisenman, Peter, 130

Electricity consumption, 65, 148

Electrostatic air filter, 27–28

Emory University, 173

Energy Star rating, 87

Energy usage
  buildings *vs.* cars/trucks, 65
  construction *vs.* occupancy,
    92–93
  efficiency, 24–25, 95
  greenwashing, 194
  reduction, green buildings,
    148
  savings, green schools, 180
Environmental benefits, exaggerated
  building size, 76
  CFLs *vs.* incandescent bulbs,
    73–74
  corporate profits, 77
  escalating consumption, 77
  farmland loss, 73
  glazed window sashes, 74–75
  green building, as oxymoron,
    72–73
  LEDs, 74
  LEED, 76
  old growth wood, 73, 75–76,
    199
  overpopulation, 76
  PVC, in windows, 76
  recycling materials, 73
  retrofitting existing buildings,
    72
Environmental Building News
  (periodical), 125
Environmental Health Fund, 190
Environmental impact
  buildings, 65, 67, 76
  footprint, large houses, 93
  green homes/communities, 30
  greenwashing, 195–196
  indoor air quality, 26–29
  large home damage, 91
  low density development, 101
  of pollution, 28
  urban sprawl costs, 101, 105–
    106
  world issues, 23

Environmental Protection Agency
  (EPA)
  allergies, 28
  CFLs, 74
  green homes, 28
  IAQ, 19
  VOCs, 49, 51
Environmental Tobacco Smoke
  (ETS), 49
Ephemeral structures
  biomimicry, 206
  eco-homes, 204
  energy efficiency, 204
  the hooch, 207–208
  lifestyle elements, 206
  McMansions, 204
  micro-compact homes, 206
  as radical architecture, 205–
    207
  recycling material, 205
  site alteration, 205
  temporary foundations, 205
  trends, 204
Escalating consumption, 77
ETS. *See* Environmental Tobacco
  Smoke

F

Family size, larger homes, 90
Farmland loss, 73
Federal action, green building, 125
Fedrizzi, Rick, 156, 159–160, 162,
  172
Fitz, Don, 167–168
Fitzgerald Architects, 116
Florida Solar Energy Center, 30
Fluorescent bulbs. *See* compact
  fluorescent bulbs (CFLs)
Foerste, Eleanor, 113–114
Forest Stewardship Council, 163
Fossil Ridge High School, 179
Four-R's: *Reduce, Recycle, Renew-
  able and Rethinking*, 24

Fraud/misrepresentation, eco-architecture, 45
Fred Hutchinson Cancer Research Center, 35–36
Freedom Tower, 70
FXFOWLE (architectural firm), 51

G

General Electric (GE), 194, 197, 200
Glazed window sashes, 74–75
Global Green USA, 181
Global warming, 72, 201
Gottfried, David, 159–160
Government. *See* State/local government(s)
Gray water, 25, 67
Great Seneca Creek Elementary, 179
Green building, difficulty of
    architecture schools, 124
    biomimicry, 125–126
    cabal-like language, 125–126
    carbon dioxide, 128
    corporate leadership, 125
    costs, 125
    cultural/structural resistance, 125
    federal action, 125
    learning curve, 125
    planning freedom, 126
    research/funding lack, 125
    talent need, 125, 126
    trade magazines, 124
    trade-offs, 125
    unsuccessful efforts, 124
    USGBC, 124–125
Green building, ease of
    commissioning fee, 119
    construction programs, 118
    cost analysis, 120
    first cost *vs.* life cycle cost, 116–117
    government involvement, 119–120
    LEED certification, 115–116, 118, 122
    planning, 117
    return on investment, 119
    square foot costs, 117
    sustainability choices, 118
    technology, 121
    US government, as landowner, 120–121
    zero net effective cost increase, 117
Green buildings
    construction programs, 118
    consumer interest, 113
    costs, 69, 113
    deep, 75
    defining, 167
    design *vs.* academic architecture, 130–131
    effectiveness of, 66
    government support, 68–69
    impact of, 47
    as oxymoron, 72–73
    performance data, 51
    resistance to, 69–70
    See also Green homes/communities
Green education, 180–183
Green Guide for Health Care (GGHC.org), 188–189
Green homes/communities, basics of
    active materials, 23
    air pollution test kits, 27
    allergies, 27–28
    automobile dependence, 32
    buying reasons, 23–24
    community ties, 30–32
    costs, 30–32
    CPSC, 28
    electrostatic air filter, 27–28
    energy efficiency, 24–25

environmental problems, 23, 28

EPA, 28

Four-R's, 24

gray-water, 25

heat-exchangers, 27

IAQ, 21

indoor environmental quality, 26–29

landscaping, 26

lead poison, 19, 27

OTA, 23–24

pollution, 28

reduced environmental impact, 30

resource consumption, 24

site respect, 29–30

sustainability, 21–23

waste materials, 23

water efficiency, 25–26

See also Green building

Green Press Initiative, 182

Greenhouse emissions, 92

Greenpeace, 195–196

Greenwashing, as challenge

corporate image transformation, 197–198

corporate reaction, 198–200

energy usage, 194

environmental impact, 193, 195–196

false claims, 196

global warming, 201

oil tankers, 196–197

rules for detecting, 198

Growth/expansion, LEED, 161

H

Hagan, Susannah, 130

Hamerschlag Hall, 174–175

Hansen, James, 128

Harvey Mudd College, 171

Hawken, Paul, 121

Hawthorne, Christopher, 129–136

Healthcare Without Harm, 188

Healthy Home Initiative, 19

Heat-exchangers, 27

Heinfeld, Dan, 67–68

Helena (apartment building), 51

Heliostat deflecting mirrors, 36

Herbert Lewis Kruse Blunck (architect firm), 117, 119

Herman Miller Marketplace, 117

Hertz, David, 133–135

Holcombe, Randall G., 97–103

Holowka, Taryn, 147–154

Home Depot, 194, 199

Homeowners' associations (HOAs)

architectural review committees, 139

clotheslines, 140–142

covenants, 143–144

home size increases, 142

penalties, 144

policies, 139

private property rights, 146

prohibitions, 140

restrictive covenants, 139

solar panels, 138, 145

square footage mandates, 141

state intervention, 144–145

xeriscaping, 141–142

The hooch, 207–208

Horn, Don, 161

Hospital for a Healthy Environment, 189

Hospitals, eco-friendly safety in

air quality/pollution, 187

building design, 191

building materials, 190

carbon dioxide release, 191

environmental standards, 189

financial savings, 190–192

GGHC.org, 188–189

government pressure, 187–188

PVC, 187–188

safety responsibility, 188–190

toxin reduction, 186–187

VOCs, 187

Howard, Bion, 21–32

I

Improvement process, 151

Indoor air quality (IAQ)

EPA, 19

ETS, 49

green design, 21, 51

LEED, 49

SBS, 45–47

student performance, 180

ventilation, 27

vs. outdoor air quality, 19

See also Air quality/pollution, indoor

Indoor Environmental Quality (IEQ), 49–51

Infrastructure costs, 31, 98

Insulating value, straw bale, 87

Interface Flooring Systems, 121

J

Johnson, Elliot, 114

Jones Lang LaSalle (architectural firm), 122

Journal of Industrial Ecology, 92, 126

Just a Dream (Van Allsburg), 182

K

Kaiser Permanente Modesto Medical Center, 188

Kaplan, Seth, 158

Kaye, Jeffrey, 64–70

Kibler, Karen, 182

Kubani, Dean, 68–69

L

Land preservation, 108–109

Land use *vs.* population growth, 108

Landro, Laura, 186–192

Landscape fragmentation, urban sprawl, 106

Landscaping, 26

Lang, Elise, 79–88

Large houses, as eco-friendly

air circulation, 87

double-pane doors/windows, 87

Eco-Manor, 86

Energy Star rating, 87

insulating value, straw bale, 87

plaster, native red clay, 85

reclaimed bead board, 86

salvaged wood, 86

straw bale construction, 79–88

truth window, 79

Large houses, not eco-friendly

carbon dioxide, 91–92

concrete, manufacture/ transportation of, 91

demolition permits, 94–95

energy efficiency/usage, 92–93, 95

environmental impact, 91, 93

family size, 90

greenhouse emissions, 92

LEED, 96

living space, per resident, 90

lumber usage, 91–92

mortgage rates, 93–94

NAHB, 90

non-rental vacation houses, 90–91

PVC usage, 92

square footage growth, 93–94

teardown economics, 95

three bathroom houses, 90

WWPA, 91

The Last Straw (periodical), 81, 83

Lawrence Berkeley National Laboratory, 47–48

LCA. *See* Life Cycle Analysis

Lead poison, 19, 27

Leadership in Energy and Environmental Design (LEED)
aid to greener buildings, 152–153
building size restriction, 76
cabal-like language, 125–126
certification, 44, 115–116, 118, 122
commissioning fee, 119
flaws, 44
government involvement, 119–120
green schools, 185
guideline utilization, 37
IEQ, 49
large houses, 96
liability exposure, 43
stated goal, 41
USGBC, 178
zero net effective cost increase, 117
See also U.S. Green Building Council

Leadership in Energy and Environmental Design (LEED), aid to greener buildings
air pollution, 148
APs, 153–154
buildings/projects, 149–150
carbon dioxide emissions, 148
certification, 150–153
cost *vs.* conventional construction, 148
discharge rate, hospitals, 149
document submission, 153
electricity consumption, 148
energy use reduction, 148
government commitment, 150
improvement process, 151
indoor living percentage, 148
LCA, 151–152

online project registration, 152
project tracking, 153
rating system, 150
raw material usage, 148
registration fees, 153
sustainability approach, 150
USGBC, 149, 150
Version 3.0, 150
water usage, 148

Leadership in Energy and Environmental Design (LEED), not effective
certification cost, 157
competing programs, 160
government adaptation, 161
growth/expansion, 161
point system, 157–158
program results, 159
PVC systems, 163
rating system, 156
registered projects, 157
Seattle requirements, 161–162
site consideration, 158
wood systems, 163

Leapfrog development, 98–99

Learning curve, green building, 125

LEED. *See* Leadership in Energy and Environmental Design (LEED)

Liability, eco-architecture, 40, 42–45

The Life and Times of a Drop of Water (Royston), 182

Life Cycle Analysis (LCA), 151–152

Light bulbs. *See* compact fluorescent bulbs (CFLs)

Light emitting diodes (LEDs), 74

Litigation, SBS, 48–49

Living roof, 171, 174

Living space, per resident, 90

Low density/single dimensional development, 98, 101

Low-income housing, aesthetics, 132–133

Ludwick, Ted, 152

Lumber usage, home construction, 91–92

Luna, Gene, 177

M

Manufacturers warranties, 43

Market forces, 103

Marmot, Alexi, 52–59

Martinkus, Ingrida, 121

Mattera, Philip, 193–202

McCorkle, Philip H., 192

McDonough, William, 125

McGee, Daniel, 69–70

McMansions, 204

Mendenhall, Brett, 117

Michael, Tim, 176

Micro-compact homes, 206

Middlebury College, 171

Moje, Bob, 180

Mortgage rates, 93–94

Musica, Frank, 40–45

N

Nabhan, Gary Paul, 173–174

National Aeronautics and Space Administration (NASA), 128

National Association of Home Builders (NAHB), 90, 158

National Center for Healthy Housing, 20

National Hanging Out Day, 141

National Resources Defense Council, 197–198

National Science Foundation, 176

Natural daylight, 36–37

Natural Resources Defense Council (NRDC), 30, 65–66

New House, 174

Non-profit status, USGBC, 160

Non-rental vacation houses, 90–91

North American Coalition on Green Building, 158

Northern Arizona University, 173

O

Office of Mobile Design, 135

Office of Technology Assessment (OTA), 23–24

Old-growth wood, 73, 75–76, 199

Ove Arup (engineering firm), 126

P

Pacific Gas & Electric (PG&E), 74

Paint, low VOC, 36

Park, Michael, 63

Pearce, Mick, 126

Penalties, HOAs, 144

Perry, Bill, 83

Photovoltaic panels, 35

Physical symptoms, SBS, 53

Piedmont Project, 173

Pierce, Michael, 79–88

Plaster, native red clay, 85

Point system, LEED, 157–158

Pollution
    air, outdoor, 105
    automobile/truck, 24, 28, 32
    environmental, 28
    HOAs, 143
    hospitals, 187
    LEED, 158
    SBS, 48
    See also Air quality/pollution

Polyvinyl chloride (PVC)
    construction usage, 92
    eco-friendly houses, 92

in hospitals, 187–188
in windows, 76
Pope, Carl, 104–110
Population growth *vs.* land use, 108
Portland State University, 170
Powell, Jane, 71–77
Private property rights, 146
Professional Remodeler (magazine), 20
Program results, LEED, 159
Project Big Green, 194
Psychosocial characteristics, SBS, 53, 55, 58–59
Pugh + Scarpa (architectural firm), 132
PVC. *See* Polyvinyl chloride

Q

Quality-of-life issues, urban sprawl, 106

R

Radical architecture, 205–207
Rahaim, John, 161–162
Rating system, LEED, 150, 156
Raw material usage, buildings, 148
Recycled materials, 136, 205
Registered projects, LEED, 157
Renewal/revitalization efforts, 109
Residential buildings. *See* buildings, commercial/residential
Resource consumption, 24
Restrictive covenants, HOAs, 139
Retrofitting existing buildings, 72
Return on investment, green design, 119
Rollens, Patrick W., 115–122
Roofs. *See* living roof
Royston, Angela, 182

S

Salas, Glen, 20
Savitsky, Jean, 122
SBS. *See* sick building syndrome (SBS) entries
Scheer, Jo, 203–208
Schendler, Auden, 123–128, 156–158
School districts, as eco-friendly benefits, 179–181
energy savings, 180
financial benefits, 183
green education, 180–183
IAQ, 180
LEED, 183–185
physical condition, 180
VOCs, 179
Seattle requirements, LEED, 161–162
Seydel, Laura Turner, 86
Seydel, Rutherford, 86
Sheer, Jo, 203–208
Sick building syndrome (SBS), as job stress symptom
building properties and SBS, 53
lack of definition, 53–54
management considerations, 59
psychosocial *vs.* physical environments, 53, 55, 58–59
research methods, 57–58
symptoms, 53
ventilation systems, 54–55
working environment, 53–54, 58
Sick building syndrome (SBS), elimination of
allergies, 48
American office workers and, 47–48
BRI, 50
commercial/residential resource usage, 47

gender-related symptoms, 57
green building impact, 47, 51
IEQ improvement, 49–51
litigation, 48–49
VOC materials and, 49
Siegal, Jennifer, 135–136
Smart-growth options/policies, 100, 107–109
Social cost reductions, 42
Society for College and University Planning, 172
Solar technology
    banning by HOAs, 138, 140, 145
    college buildings, 174, 179
    grants, 73
    low-income apartments, 132–133
    passive, 25, 29, 126
    photovoltaic panels, 35, 66, 68–70
    single family homes, 134
    solatubes, 75, 86
    state laws, 144
    Syndecrete, 135
Southern Building Code, 83
Square footage issues, green building, 93–94, 117, 141
Standard of living, low density development, 101
Stang, Alanna, 129–136
State/local government(s)
    green building support, 68–69
    hospitals, eco-friendly safety, 187–188
    LEED, 150, 161
    urban sprawl, 102, 106–107, 110
Steen, Athena, 81
Steen, Bill, 81
Stern, Robert A. M., 124
Stone, James, 136
Straw bale home
    air circulation, 87

benefits, 78
construction codes, 82
fire tests, 83
humidity concerns, 81, 84
insulating value, 87
large houses, 79–88
semipermeable coatings, 85
storage, 84
truth window, 79
wood usage, 84
The Straw Bale House (Steen and Steen), 81
Strip/ribbon development, 98–100
Sulfur dioxide, 65
Sunshade prisms, 36
Surface area exposure, large houses, 93
Sustainability
    advantages, 38
    architects, 131
    choices, 118
    college campuses, 171–172
    design standards, 40–41
    of green homes, 21–23
    LEED approach, 150
    USGBC, 37–38
Sustainable Forestry Initiative, 163
Sustainable Solutions Corporation, 19
Switzer, Howard, 82, 85
Syndecrete, 133, 135

T

Tankless water heater, 25–26
Taylor, Thomas, 118
Teardown economics, 95
Technology, green building, 121
Thompson, Ventulett, Stainback and Associates (architect firm), 121
Three bathroom houses, 90
Toyota Building, 68
Toyota Motor Sales, 200

Toyota South Campus project, 37–39

Traffic, urban sprawl, 102

Transit village, small communities, 62–64

Transit Villages in the 21st Century (Bernick and Cervero), 62

Truth window, straw bale home, 79

Turner Construction, 34, 36–37, 39

U

Udall, Randy, 156–157

Uniform Commercial Code liability limitations, 42–43

United Nations Environmental Programme, 22

United Nations (UN), 90

University of Pittsburgh Medical Center, 192

University of South Carolina, 170–172, 176

Urban growth boundaries (UGBs), 109

Urban sprawl, as beneficial
advantages, 99
affordability, 98
commuting patterns, 102
costs, 99
decentralized growth, 102–103
environmental impact, 101, 105–106
infrastructure, 98
leapfrog development, 98–99
local government role, 102
low density/single dimensional development, 98, 101
market forces, 103
planning/development, 98–99
standard of living, 101
street right-of-ways, 100
streetscapes, 100

strip/ribbon development, 98–100
traffic, 102
zoning laws, 101

Urban sprawl, not beneficial
costs, 105–106
decentralized development, 109–110
government subsidies, 106–107, 110
land preservation, 108–109
land use *vs.* population growth, 108
landscape fragmentation, 106
local policies, 105
quality-of-life issues, 106
renewal/revitalization efforts, 109
smart growth options, 107–109
UGBs, 109
vegetation/soil loss, 106

U.S. Climate Action Partnership, 198

U.S. Green Building Council (USGBC)
colleges certified, 171
first cost *vs.* life cycle cost, 117
founding, 149
glazed window sashes, 75
growth, 124–125
member concerns, 162
non-profit status, 160
sustainability, 37–38
See also Leadership in Energy and Environmental Design

U.S. resource usage, 23

US government, as landowner, 120–121

V

Van Allsburg, Chris, 182

Vegetation/soil loss, urban sprawl, 106

Version 3.0, LEED, 150

Volatile organic compounds (VOCs)
    building products, 19
    EPA, 49, 51
    in hospitals, 187
    low emissions from, 36
    SBS and, 49
    in schools, 179

W

Wal-Mart, 199
Walsh, Bill, 160
Warranties, green buildings, 44–45
Washington State University, 175
Waste materials, green homes, 23
Water efficiency/usage, 25–26, 148
Water-miser appliance, 25
Watson, Rob, 65–67
West Quad, 176–177
Western Wood Products Association (WWPA), 91
Whelan, Debra Lau, 178–185
White, William, 83
Wille, Rod F., 33–39

Wood usage
    carbon dioxide, 92
    old-growth, 73, 75–76, 199
    salvaged, 86
    straw bale homes, 84
    systems, 163
Working environment, 54, 58
World Health Organization, 47
World Resources Institute, 194
WWPA. *See* Western Wood Products Association

X

Xeriscaping, 141–142

Y

Yayapai College, 171

Z

Zero net effective cost increase, 117
Zoning laws, single-dimensional development, 101